A Place to Live, to Love, to Learn

A Memoir of
The Founding of The Angelus

A Place to Live, to Love, to Learn

A Memoir of
The Founding of The Angelus

PAULINE NERI SHAVER

with

PERRI NERI

A Place to Live, to Love, to Learn: A Memoir of
The Founding of The Angelus

ISBN: 978-1-967674-12-1 (Paperback)
ISBN: 978-1967674-13-8 (eBook)
Library of Congress Control Number: 2025916542

Book Cover Design: OKOMATO
Interior Design: Amit Dey
Editor: Winsome Hudson
Pauline Author Photo Credit: Perri Neri
Perri Neri Photo Credit: Danny Bristoll
Photo Section Credit: Compliments of the Family with permissions
from photographers where applicable.

Website: www.wordeee.com
Twitter.com/wordeeeupdates
Facebook: facebook.com/Wordeee/
e-mail: contact@wordeee.com
Published by Wordeee in the United States, New York,
New York 2025

DISCLOSURE

The Angelus is a real organization founded and led by the author of this book. Throughout these pages, its name is used openly and with great care to honor its legacy and the community it served. Although the name of the group home is shared, the individuals mentioned in the stories have had their names and identifying details altered to protect their privacy. In some cases, composite characters and adapted events are used to further ensure confidentiality. The stories are drawn from personal memory and are shared from the perspective of lived experience, not as medical records or clinical documentation. Our intent is to preserve the heart and humanity of these moments while respecting the dignity and privacy of all involved.

For my beloved husband,
Dave, my children, Joe, Perri and Marty,
and my grandchildren, Joelle, Tori, Nick, and Julie.

ADVANCE PRAISE

"This book gives a voice to those longing to be heard and shares a message of love meant to be lived, shared, and echoed by all. Through its tender memories and honest reflections, it honors the strength of unbroken spirits. It's a testament to resilience, reminding us that hope endures, strength prevails, and every life is worth celebrating."

—Pam Peone,
Board Member, The Angelus

"I love this place. The Angelus is my home."

—Tom B.
Resident at The Angelus

"Words cannot adequately express my admiration and love for Pauline Neri Shaver. She has created a beautiful country home and a life of dignity, joy, and fellowship for individuals with significant disabilities. Her example of love and respect for the residents continues to inspire the current generation, whose dedication makes the Angelus the blessing it is and has always been."

—Catherine M. Giangreco, MD
Retired Physician and parent of an Angelus resident

"What an inspiration. The Angelus has truly been a place to live, to love, to learn for over the last four decades and will continue...."

—Joe Neri

"Over 30 years ago, meeting Pauline at The Angelus changed my life. Her story in *A Place to Live, to Love, to Learn: A Memoir of the Founding of The Angelus* shows the power of one person's vision to create a community filled with love and compassion. Pauline will always be my hero. "Reading this memoir is like walking those grounds yourself and witnessing the difference one determined person can make. Pauline has been, and will always be, my hero."

—Tammy Williams,
Event Coordinator, The Angelus

"Pauline Neri Shaver's legacy isn't just in the walls she built, but in the lives she transformed. *A Place to Live, to Love, to Learn: A Memoir of the Founding of The Angelus* shows how one woman's dream became a movement."

—Kirk Morten,
Friend and Marketing Director

"The Angelus is a 'gift'. It is a testimony to the best sentiments and actions of the human heart. Working with Pauline, individuals from all walks of life had the ability to provide for the most vulnerable children, men, and women. Together, it was a quest of love and selflessness.

— Elaine Tomasch Neri, M.Ed.

FOREWORD

I will never forget the day I met Pauline Neri.

It was 1984. I was 18 years old and thrilled to see a job posting in the newspaper. I applied right away, and Pauline herself interviewed me. I got the job, and looking back now, I realize what a gift that opportunity truly was.

I come from a family of five children, and I'm the second youngest. My oldest sister was born with a cleft palate and brain damage caused by a staph infection at birth. When I was just three years old, my sister was sent to live in a state institution at the age of ten. It was a devastating moment for our entire family, one that shaped much of how I came to understand love, loss, and the importance of compassionate care. I believe Pauline recognized that early awareness and depth of understanding when we met, even though I was just 18 at the time. She also knew my father, who was then the President and CEO of PARC, an organization much like The Angelus, devoted to serving children and adults with disabilities. Maybe that gave her a little extra confidence in hiring me. Whatever the reason, that day changed my life.

Pauline became one of the greatest teachers I've ever had, not in a classroom, but in the everyday acts of caregiving. She taught me the difference between simply meeting someone's physical needs and truly connecting with them. Her way of caring was deeply personal and profoundly respectful. She saw everyone for who they were inside, and she made sure they knew they mattered.

At the time, I remember being struck by the enormity of what she was doing. She had dedicated her life to helping children who, in many cases, no one else wanted. Some had been left at state institutions and forgotten by their families. Pauline didn't accept that. She believed every child deserved love, dignity, and a home, not just a place to stay. And she was determined to make that happen. She began with a small home in South St. Petersburg, caring for just a few children. But her vision grew, and she transformed that humble beginning into something extraordinary: a peaceful, welcoming retreat on several acres of land in Hudson, Florida. The Angelus became more than a place to live. It became a place to belong.

This memoir is a beautiful, honest reflection of that journey. Pauline, with her daughter Perri by her side as co-author, has captured not just the history of The Angelus, but its soul. Through these pages, you'll meet the people who helped make the dream a reality, from caregivers to country music legends, volunteers to visionaries. You'll read about the sacrifices, the setbacks, and the triumphs. But more than anything, you'll feel the love that made it all possible.

Reading this book brought me back to those early days at The Angelus. My own journey since then has been diverse, taking me through different places and roles, but today I serve as the President and CEO of the Parc Center for Disabilities. I truly believe that the seeds Pauline planted in me all those years ago are what led me here, continuing in my own way to help humanity with compassion, purpose, and hope.

If you're holding this book, you're about to experience something special. Pauline's story is not just a chronicle of one woman's mission. It's an invitation to believe in what's possible when faith, purpose, and compassion come together. So, take a deep breath, turn the page, and let yourself be moved. I know you will be.

Michelle Detweiler
President & CEO
Parc Center for Disabilities
St. Petersburg, FL

TABLE OF CONTENTS

AUTHOR'S NOTES

I never intended to write a book. I've always believed in doing the work, not writing about it. But as the years passed and the stories built up in my heart, I began to feel that they weren't mine to hold alone anymore.

This memoir is my attempt to share what I lived, what I learned, and what I loved most deeply. The Angelus is my life's work, but more than that, it is a place where miracles—big and small—unfold every day.

When I first began this journey, I could never have imagined how profoundly it would transform me. The Angelus started as a simple idea, born from heartbreak, hope, and a desire to help. But it became so much more. It became a sanctuary, not just for children with complex needs, but for all of us lucky enough to care for them. Over the years, The Angelus has grown into a home where every story matters, where every life shines in its own remarkable way.

The stories in this book are drawn from my memories. They are deeply personal reflections of the moments that shaped me. Stories of joy, heartbreak, growth, and resilience. They tell of children who were labeled, underestimated, or cast aside, only to flourish when given the love and care they deserved. Their names and certain details have been changed to protect their privacy, but the spirit of their stories remains true.

The Angelus is more than a place; it is a quilt, stitched together by the lives of those who have called it home. Each patch represents a unique story, a different life, a new challenge faced with compassion, love, and laughter. Whether it's a child's uncontainable joy while taking their first roll across the carpet, or a young athlete with an indomitable spirit earning a gold medal at the Special Olympics, these stories reflect the quiet miracles that unfold every day.

This book is a tribute to them. It is a reminder of what happens when we look beyond labels and see the human spirit in its fullest light. I hope that as you read, you will feel the laughter echoing through our halls, the tears that fell in difficult times, and the joy of witnessing lives filled with possibility. May these stories inspire you to see the extraordinary in the ordinary and to believe, as I do, that one person can make a difference, even if that difference begins with a single step.

This is my story, and theirs, woven together. I write this with gratitude for the people who trusted me, stood beside me, and reminded me that even one person, with no experience but a heart wide open, can help change lives.

—Pauline Neri Shaver

This book began, as many important things do, with a conversation between mother and daughter. As my mother and I looked back on the early days of The Angelus, we found ourselves rediscovering moments of grace, love, strength, and yes, humor that had long lived quietly in our memories. What started as storytelling soon grew into a deeper collaboration: A Place to Live, to Love, to Learn: A Memoir the Founding of The Angelus. While this isn't a traditional memoir, I believe you will understand my mother through the work she dedicated her life to.

While these pages herein reflect Pauline's voice and experiences, I was proud to help bring them forward; to listen, to ask questions, to write and rewrite with care. Some stories emerged from memory, others from notes and archives, and many from the heart. It was a privilege to walk beside my mother in retelling them.

—Perri Neri

PART ONE

BUILDING HOPE:
BIRTH OF THE ANGELUS

"I've lived a life that might seem ordinary from the outside, but it's been full of extraordinary moments. I guess, deep down, I always believed that if you've been given a lot, you ought to give something back."

I was born in 1937 in West Warwick, Rhode Island, the youngest of four children of Florence and Horace Cadoret. From the age of four to twelve, I attended a boarding school run by nuns—something not unusual at the time for Catholic families of means. While some might find that surprising, I truly loved it. The structure suited me, even if I didn't always follow the rules. I was a bit mischievous, but I was well-loved by the sisters. On annual Coronation Days, which parents attended, the girls wearing white dresses indicated they'd been good all year, and those in black dresses had not. Once, when I was in black, my father caught my eye from his seat, winked, and mouthed, "That-a-girl," with a glint of pride and understanding. It's a memory that still makes me smile.

Those early years taught me discipline, determination, and perhaps most importantly, how to find joy and connection even in the midst of rules and routine. I carried those lessons with me throughout my life—into my work, into motherhood, and into building a home and community at The Angelus.

Thinking back, one of the people who influenced me most was my sister-in-law, Yvette. I didn't witness it myself—in fact, I only came to know the full story much later, in the kind of heart-to-heart talks you have when you're looking back on life. For seven years, Yvette worked at a state hospital in Massachusetts, caring for eight adult men with intellectual and developmental disabilities. She called them her "gentle giants" — big, strong men who had spent most of their lives in an institution. On her very first day, one of them accidentally broke her arm. Most people would have walked away, but not Yvette. She showed up the very next morning, cast and all, and kept showing up for years. She wasn't afraid. She gave her heart to that work, and in time, they grew to trust and love her.

That kind of courage and commitment made a lasting impression on me. Hearing about her care for people who were so often misunderstood and overlooked planted something in me: the belief that everyone deserves dignity, patience, and a place to belong. I may not have realized it at the time, but her example helped shape the work I would later do at The Angelus.

I didn't set out to start an organization for children in need. I wasn't a parent of a child with disabilities. But when I met a child whose circumstances opened my eyes to an overwhelming need, I felt God calling me to do something about it, and I couldn't turn away.

In the early years, there were no clear paths, just prayer, persistence, and a sense that this work was bigger than me. Families were desperate for help, and children with profound needs had few options. The Angelus began as a response to that need, grounded in my Catholic faith and sustained by a belief that every life has purpose, no matter how complex the challenges.

Over time, The Angelus became a haven, not just a place of care, but of love, learning, and belonging. My story is part of a larger movement of faith-driven service, community building, and advocacy for those too often overlooked. It's a story of saying yes to something hard and holy, and trusting that grace would do the rest.

Yes, I like the word "yes." I see myself as someone who says "yes" when it would have been easier to say "no." I wasn't the most qualified, the most experienced, or the most prepared, but I was willing. Over the years, I've grown from a woman full of questions and self-doubt into someone who has found strength in faith and purpose. I see myself now not just as a caregiver or a founder, but as a witness to the extraordinary power of love when it is put into action.

I was a single parent of three school-age children when I applied for a job at our local Catholic school, where my children were enrolled. Being able to watch over them while I found a way to support us was a burden lifted. Father Goodman, the priest in charge of the parish and school, offered me a position as a physical education teacher, and I eagerly accepted.

At the time, thank goodness, PE teachers weren't required to have a degree. I jumped in with both feet pretending I knew exactly what I was doing. To educate myself about what I had just accepted to do, become a PE teacher, I headed straight to the library and gathered every resource I could find. With these resources, I pulled together lesson plans and built an exercise and sports program for grades 1 through 8.

It turned out to be the perfect job! Being at the school my children attended while immersing myself in something new was fulfilling.

I started an after-school program and fell in love with learning about different sports and games. I introduced basketball, volleyball, track, and kickball, and between seasons, I added the Presidential Physical Fitness Program and classic yard games. Father Goodman later hired a young college graduate named Tom to teach history and PE for the 7th and 8th-grade boys. Tom was a natural fit for our coed after-school program, which grew into a big success. Both the boys' and girls' teams won championships across multiple sports, bringing pride and excitement to the school.

After ten years of working under the Florida sun and with my own children now grown and chasing their dreams, I felt it was time for a change. During my years at the school, I had met many families struggling with the complexities of parent-child relationships, as well as children dealing with personal challenges. I began to imagine a different kind of place, a farm where kids could take a break, step away from their family struggles and find a sense of peace. To prepare for this new path, I enrolled in a behavior modification course. During that course, I met a young girl who would quietly shift the entire direction of my life.

Amber, a child with physical and visual impairments, was brought to the class by two caretakers who did not have anyone to care for her while they were away. From the start it was clear that she understood far more than people assumed. She tilted her head to see what was happening and I often caught her expressions changing in response to conversation; her smile arriving right on cue with a funny story, sadness falling across her face when someone spoke about her as if she weren't there.

She wasn't just listening. She was feeling every word. Her situation troubled me deeply. I learned that the home she was in wasn't built to accommodate her needs. Each day she had to be carried up and downstairs in her wheelchair. Worse, I came to understand that she had no permanent placement; the next option for her was likely a large facility not designed for children.

I had entered that class hoping to prepare for working with children in crisis. But after meeting Amber, my focus changed. God had another plan for me. My vision began to shift. I no longer felt called to help children with their family struggles. I wanted to create a real home for children with physical challenges who needed consistent care and a chance to thrive. A place where they could be seen and known.

I didn't know anything about caring for people with disabilities. But I did know Amber needed help, and I couldn't turn away from that. Even though the path was unsure, I had the feeling of being called to do something meaningful. So, just like when I figured out how to be a good PE. Teacher and coach, I knew that if I showed up and did what needed to be done, one step at a time, things would come together. The idea that ordinary people can do extraordinary things when they act with faith, compassion, and courage was my guiding light.

I began researching everything I could about what services were available to Amber. What I discovered shocked me: there were no licensed group homes in Florida dedicated to children with complex physical needs. If I wanted such a place to exist, I would have to build it myself. Meeting Amber opened my eyes. I saw how much she was struggling, and how little was out there for a child like her. The Angelus, born out of that meeting, didn't start with a grand plan—it started with a "yes" to helping one child. I responded to a need, followed where love led, and trusted that things would fall into place.

I started by selling my little house in Gulfport and buying a larger one in St. Petersburg, one that could become a true home for the children. At the same time, I was navigating the demanding process of meeting the state's licensing requirements. To make it all possible, I worked overnight shifts as a medical transcriptionist. Each report I typed was another step toward raising the necessary funds to realize my mission. I was juggling exhaustion, precision, and purpose, never losing sight of the vision. The home, the license, the future; it was all for the children I knew were coming.

Then the rigorous process of meeting the criteria for licensing began. There were no templates for a group home for disabled children, so I could only prepare to meet the requirements for the generic group home model. For example, each bedroom had to have the correct square footage, a mirror, a towel bar, and two dresser drawers. There were no criteria that addressed the needs of a child with physical disabilities.

I also had to ensure that there was enough money in the bank to sustain the home in case government funding was delayed. My three siblings bravely lent me their inheritance from our Aunt Cecile Cadoret's will, which I deposited in my bank account for two months, just long enough to meet the licensing criteria. The money was returned to them in full, without interest, and I remain deeply grateful for their trust and generosity. Additionally, while a degree wasn't required, I felt some college credits could possibly help strengthen the application.

Throughout my years as a PE teacher my best friend had been a nun, Sister Nicole (pronounced Nickel-ay). She had entered the convent right out of high school and for seventeen years was a part of the order. She had moved back to Ohio by then, but we stayed in close touch while I was still teaching.

I shared my story about Amber and my new purpose with her. Sister Nicole was intrigued by it all and eventually she received permission to leave her religious community and reenter the secular world. Retaining her birth name, Elaine, in February 1979, she arrived in St. Petersburg to help me build this very special and much needed group home. Together we transformed the house, decorating the bedrooms with colorful bedspreads and cheerful curtains. We poured our hearts into every detail, knowing this wasn't just a house, it was going to be a home.

When it came time to name our new residence, we thought back to our days teaching at Holy Name and found inspiration in Father Goodman. Every morning before school, he would lead us in saying The Angelus, which is a traditional Catholic prayer about the birth of Christ. It's meant to be said in the morning, at noon, and again at night. That rhythm reminded me of the kind of care we hoped to give our residents: steady and loving; morning, noon, and night. We named it The Angelus. And so, The Angelus was born.

With the house ready, we began reviewing support plans developed by social workers from the Health and Rehabilitative Services (HRS). They were often tasked with finding placement for children with severe disabilities. And with our licensure in place, they finally had an option for placing non-ambulatory placements with Cerebral Palsy into a group home, and not into a state facility or nursing home. As Elaine and I looked through the paperwork, one name stood out, Angela—a name that would be the first step in turning The Angelus into what it was meant to be.

The journey had started with a simple job in a school gymnasium. It evolved through moments of inspiration, unexpected encounters, and an unwavering belief that every child deserves a place where they are safe, seen, and valued. Looking back, I never could have imagined that saying "yes" to a PE teaching job would set me on the path to something far greater. But The Angelus wasn't just built on plans and paperwork; it was built on faith, determination, and a deep commitment to making sure that children like Amber never had to wonder if they were truly wanted.

And with that, the doors to The Angelus opened. The real story was just beginning.

PERRI:
A CREATIVE LEGACY OF LOVE

My daughter Perri is the heart of so many cherished moments at The Angelus. She has been a constant source of love, creativity, and support throughout the years. Her name appears in countless stories about our residents because she has been instrumental in nurturing not just the growth of our community, but the very spirit. An artist and hairstylist by trade, Perri was always just a phone call away. Whether I needed help at a moment's notice or a burst of creative inspiration, she was there. As our social director, she transformed every gathering into a celebration. One of her most memorable contributions was a painting activity that included finger paints and large sheets of poster board.

It was a warm summer day, and the children were in their bathing suits ready to play in the sprinklers. But first, Perri laid the poster boards down onto the grass, poured the finger paints, and you can imagine what happened next. The children joyfully rolled in the paint using their bodies to create vibrant, one-of-a-kind body painting masterpieces! What fun!

Perri was also our personal hairstylist, bringing out smiles with every snip and style. I still remember the time when she gave Amber her very first perm, turning her into a little lamb with adorable curls. Ever inventive, Perri also crafted unique costumes for each resident, accompanying them to school Halloween events and turning ordinary days into unforgettable adventures.

Her caring nature shone through even in the practical moments of our lives. Perri helped me take two of our young residents to Jacksonville for a Special Olympics competition, an experience they never forgot. She also helped me take them to their first time seeing a live–theater performance and the joy on their faces is something I'll always remember.

There was even a time when she moved in to provide overnight support, ensuring that every morning at The Angelus began with warmth, dignity, and a sense of readiness for the day ahead. She balanced helping me at The Angelus with her work as a hairstylist and cosmetology instructor, and I couldn't imagine the early years without the generosity of her spirit.

Perri eventually moved on to pursue a Fine Arts degree at the University of Tampa and was then accepted into the MFA program at Pratt Institute in New York. Even from New York City, Perri remained deeply connected to our community. Every year she poured her heart into creating our annual Christmas cards, each one a beautiful blend of family, residents, and holiday magic. Over time, these cards have evolved into a treasured tradition. At The Angelus' Christmas light show, you will see large wooden panels, hand-painted reproductions of her Christmas cards illuminated by white lights, symbolizing the warmth and unity she helped foster.

Finally, Perri played an essential role in bringing this book together. From afar, she meticulously edited our stories and helped me recall the fine details of the trials and joys we experienced in St. Pete as we built The Angelus, and in Hudson, where we continued to grow.

ANGELA:
A JOURNEY OF GROWTH
AND INDEPENDENCE

Angela was the very first child to come to The Angelus in early 1979. She was six years old, non-verbal and non-ambulatory, and had spent those six years being shuffled from one foster home to another. While reading her support plan from the state, Elaine and I learned that Angela was placed into a foster home due to early instability in her family. We also learned that she went to a Special Education school, a place for students with "special needs." Elaine and I wanted to meet her, so we planned a visit.

When we arrived, we met Angela, a bright-eyed little girl sitting in a wheelchair, surrounded by young children running around and laughing while they waited for the school bus. There were twelve children, all ambulatory, and all mainstreamed into a typical public school. Angela was the only one in a wheelchair. The woman in charge was kind, but I could see that she was overwhelmed. She explained to me how holding a spoon was challenging for Angela and how the other children often stole food from Angela's tray, leaving her without enough to eat. With so many children to attend to, Angela could not get the assistance she needed. Her solution was to lower her face to the tray and push the food into her mouth. Angela, following along with the conversation, mimicked those motions for us. "I imagine it can be pretty messy, right?" I asked Angela, who responded with a smile and a gentle wrist nod, her own version of "yes."

As we continued our conversation using a series of yes/no questions, it was clear to me that she understood every question we had. I was hoping that Angela's potential wasn't being overlooked. And it was with this gentle wrist nod that Angela told us that she wanted to come live with us at The Angelus.

The paperwork was processed quickly, and soon Angela was on her way to her new home. The Angelus house was sparse and quiet, compared to the household she just left, but it was also warm and welcoming. The living room had a beautiful stone fireplace and soft shag carpeting sprinkled with colorful bean bags. We gently lowered her onto a bean bag in the soft-carpeted living room, and with a big smile, she began to roll and wriggle in every direction, full of joy. Though she couldn't speak, she made it clear that she was excited and ready to be a part of something new. Her giggles were joyfully infectious. She was showing us, in her own way, that she could move, just not like everyone else. I knew this was the start of something special.

Angela's first day was a learning experience for all of us. For example, because she had difficulty chewing and swallowing, her food needed to be finely cut. Angela could not use a straw, and so we found ways to give her the assistance she needed to drink from a cup. She required support and supervision for bathing and by keeping the water level low, Angela could wiggle and splash, turning bath time into a scene of endless giggles. Oh, how she loved the warm water!

Angela was also the first Black child I had ever cared for, and I'll admit, I had a lot to learn. It wasn't her disability that challenged me at first; it was her hair. I didn't yet understand how to care for her tight curls or the importance of keeping her skin well-moisturized.

The learning curve was steep, but it came from a place of love. We figured it out together, slowly. Angela was patient with me, even when I was fumbling, her deep, expressive eyes told me it was all going to be okay.

The next day was a school day. And so began the morning routine of waking Angela up with a cheerful "Good morning, it's time to get up for school." I got her dressed while Elaine prepared breakfast of oatmeal with cinnamon and brown sugar, and a glass of orange juice. "Let's brush those teeth." Angela smiled and opened wide, grimacing a bit at the taste of the toothpaste as Elaine brushed her teeth. A quick face wipe with a warm washcloth, and we were on our way.

Angela was not able to stand momentarily, so I picked her up out of her wheelchair and placed her safely in the car. Once she settled in and buckled up, I folded her wheelchair and placed it into the trunk. Off we went to her Special Education classroom, where the staff already knew her and were happy to see her smiling face.

As more children joined the Angelus, Angela welcomed each one, creating a sense of family. She communicated quite well through expressive sounds, eye contact, facial gestures, and simple signs. Of course, she used her wrist nod for yes, and a head shake accompanied by a firm "nnnoh" for no. Over time, it became clear that Angela was far more intelligent than her records suggested. I felt strongly that Angela would thrive in a mainstream classroom. Elaine, with her background in education, arranged for Angela to be retested. The results opened new doors for her! She now had the chance to be included in activities with verbal and ambulatory classmates and was transferred to a mainstream public school. It was a proud day for all of us.

As Angela grew, she faced new physical challenges. Her muscle stiffness worsened, and I could see how even simple movements like relaxing into a seat or shifting her posture were getting increasingly difficult. I began to explore options for relief. A cerebellar stimulator, a surgically implanted device designed to reduce muscle tightness, was recommended by her neurologist. But because it was not FDA-approved at the time, it was not covered by Medicaid or any state programs. We also had to travel to Miami for the surgery. So, with the support of her school principal, we launched a walkathon that raised more than $5,000. The remaining funds needed to make this happen were contributed by friends and family. Angela and I were off to Miami!

The plane ride itself was a thrill. Angela was practically vibrating with excitement. But getting to our seats? That was a different kind of adventure. She had grown even taller by then, and her muscles had not grown with her bones making her legs stiff and uncooperative. I couldn't transfer her directly from her wheelchair into the plane seat; there simply wasn't room. We left her chair at the door of the plane to be stowed, and I did what I had to: I stood behind her, slid my arms under hers, and helped her walk the length of the narrow aisle, half-lifting her as she moved one foot in front of the other. Each step was a negotiation between her determination and the resistance of her own body.

Her gait was awkward, legs crossing slightly, knees stiff, but she did it. She was also really excited. It was her first plane ride. I focused on the joy of the moment, saying hello to fellow passengers and, "Whoops, excuse us," both of us giggling as we bumped into every other seat along the way, knocking elbows, bags, and probably a few nerves. By the time we reached our row, both of us were flushed, breathless, and laughing at the spectacle we must have been.

Just as we were about to move into our seats, the flight attendant swooped in and gently blocked our path. "One moment," she said, unfolding a thin cotton sheet and laying it across Angela's seat. "It's for evacuation purposes," she explained. "You know, in case of an emergency, we can just scoop her up and out of the plane."

Angela tilted her head toward me and rolled her eyes dramatically. Her expression said everything: Seriously? I bit my lip to keep from laughing too loudly. Even in that moment, tired, awkward, sandwiched between strangers and stares, she held her grace, her humor, and her razor-sharp awareness of everything around her. Settled into her window seat, Angela watched the clouds with wide, excited eyes.

At the hospital, extensive testing revealed that her cognitive skills were within a good range, stronger than they had imagined. Although nervous about the surgery, Angela's strength shone through. The operation went smoothly, and adjustments to the stimulator were made by phone, our landline phone! This was before cell phones and Bluetooth technology. Simply hold the phone to the implanted device, and a series of beeps and tones would communicate with it. I remember how those sounds made Angela laugh. And I remember feeling so grateful that this new technology made a difference. The tightness in her muscles reduced noticeably, allowing Angela to participate more fully in daily activities and made getting her schoolwork done with greater ease.

Angela began using communication tools: a low-tech laminated word board, a page filled with frequently used phrases; action icons; pictures; and the alphabet for spelling. With practice, Angela became skilled at pointing at icons or letters with her eyes or a guided hand. She used this device to express needs, crack jokes, and even plan outings. Later, Angela used a more advanced version of a word board and was even invited to demonstrate her communication device at university conferences. I think that these experiences broadened her world and brought her immense joy. And I was so proud of her and so very grateful for a community that made it all possible.

A local TV station aired a story about the fundraising for her surgery. Angela squealed with excitement, waiting for the segment to come on, but after watching herself on screen, she turned solemn. When I asked her if she liked it, she responded firmly, "nnnoh." I was surprised at her reaction, but after talking to her about it, I began to understand why she was sad. It was the first time Angela had seen herself on television, and she did not like how she looked, especially the involuntary movements in her face. I remember the look in her eyes, the quiet disappointment, the vulnerability of suddenly seeing oneself through a different lens. At that moment I realized something was shifting in her. This wasn't just about a screen or an image; it was Angela grappling with what the world might see, and how that differed from how she felt inside. It's a reckoning so many of us face, regardless of ability.

I sat with her, gently reminding her of the strength it took to be on camera in the first place and the wisdom she carried in her heart. I told her what was true: that her beauty shines, not in spite of anything, but because of who she is.

As for the stimulator device, after about a year, the wiring dislodged. Without additional funding, we couldn't afford a second surgery. Angela was left with a large keloid scar and some emotional pain. She experienced a period of depression, but she carried on with a kind of steady strength, learning to navigate the loss in her own time and on her own terms. She continued to thrive in school, using a power chair and an even more sophisticated electronic communication device. She excelled in social settings, participating in concerts, camping trips, and outings. One of her most cherished experiences was attending Girl Scout camp with her housemates, where she helped staff understand the needs of her friends. At church, she used a special walker to represent people with disabilities, creating connections with members of the congregation who had previously been hesitant to approach her.

She formed deep attachments to caregivers and cried whenever someone moved on to another job or another chapter in life. Saying goodbye was always hard for Angela. Still, she forged ahead.

After many years together, and as Angela reached adulthood, she entered a program focused on developing independent living skills. I think that the idea of having her own apartment and making her own decisions excited her. Of course it did. And with the same determination and strength, Angela moved into a shared apartment with her own caregiver and began a new chapter of her life. We stayed in touch for as long as we could. Though our hearts broke when we lost contact, we remain grateful for the fifteen years with us. Angela remains etched in my heart.

CAROLINE:
A BRIEF BUT BRIGHT SPARK

Word began to spread among caseworkers that our group home was uniquely prepared to care for children with physical disabilities. The need was great. One stormy February day, we welcomed two new residents flown in from Jacksonville; one of them was Caroline, just eight years old, full of spirit and unpredictability.

The flight was turbulent, with the plane circling Tampa airport for over thirty minutes due to bad weather. Elaine and I waited anxiously at the gate, where two exhausted women emerged, each holding a child. One carried Caroline, her face red from crying, hair tangled and wild, eyes wide with emotion. There was no long farewell. The caregivers handed the children off and disappeared back into the plane.

Caroline's arrival was unforgettable, largely due to her spirited personality. Her emotions often arrived in waves—screaming one moment, laughing the next. Her behavior during the flight, I later learned, had been so disruptive that the airline offered free drinks to passengers to ease tensions. Yet, despite her rough start, Caroline quickly settled into life in our group home. I remember seeing glimpses of humor and creativity that hinted at a deeper story.

Caroline, unable to be cared for by her family, and with no suitable alternatives, was placed with us after years in a large state facility. From her very first days at The Angelus, Caroline surprised me in many ways. Caroline had a tendency to repeat phrases, with dramatic flair;

sometimes funny, sometimes unsettling. One afternoon, she slammed her hand on the table and shouted, "Clean those damned tables!" in a voice that echoed someone she had likely heard many times. It was both revealing and sobering.

I couldn't be sure of her past, but her words, behaviors, and reactions made us want to move slowly and carefully. Caroline's eating habits gave us pause. She refused food at first, barely speaking—until my son Joe walked in with a bag of French fries. Her face lit up. "Fries?" she asked softly. That was all it took. Joe handed one to her, and she eagerly reached out. In that moment, it felt like something unlocked in her. I didn't know what kind of history she had with food, but we knew it mattered.

Gradually she joined group meals and began feeding herself, first with her fingers, then with a spoon. Her laughter came more often, and her energy filled the house. Caroline didn't sit still. I remember how she scooted, rolled, and talked to herself with endless curiosity. She would often hold her hand in the air like she was catching sunlight, smiling to no one in particular. Music especially brought her peace. I noticed how she would pause, lean in, and smile in a way that made me feel it deep in my chest. Her laughter, often spontaneous and contagious, became one of the house's sweetest sounds.

After about a year, Caroline was transferred back to Jacksonville to be reunited with her mother. At the time, it was common practice for the state to prioritize family reunification. While I never knew the reasons behind the decision, I could only hope that Caroline would be safe and loved. Her time with us was brief, but unforgettable. When I think about Caroline, I think about how even brief connections can hold lasting meaning. And I think about a child who endured the weight of difficult circumstances and still found light.

JOE:
A LEGACY OF DEDICATION
AND STEADFAST STRENGTH

From the very beginning, my son Joe Neri played a vital role in supporting The Angelus. While attending airplane mechanics school, he still found time in the evenings to help feed Pete, one of our residents who had a severe swallowing disorder caused by cerebral palsy. On weekends, he was just as devoted—building and painting shelves in our garage, pouring concrete for a porch, and installing screening so the children could enjoy a safe and welcoming outdoor space. Every project he took on made our home stronger, safer, and filled with more possibilities."

After graduating, Joe and his wife, Elaine, moved to Houston, Texas. Joe got a solid job at Continental Airlines and Elaine became a school principal. A few years later they welcomed their daughter, my first grandchild, Joelle. One of the perks of Joe's job was access to standby tickets. Thanks to that, we were able to take The Angelus residents on some unforgettable trips: to Minnesota to see snow, to the Mall of America, and even to Chicago to reunite a resident with his sister.

In 1995, Joe and his family returned to Florida. He took on the role of houseparent at Florence House, home to ten of our residents. His mornings began at 5 a.m., greeting the night staff and helping residents who were fed via gastrostomy tubes (or G-tubes). Feeding tubes were necessary for several of our residents who couldn't chew or swallow safely, and administering those feedings required training.

He also ensured that each resident's Individualized Support Plan (ISP) was up to date and followed carefully. These plans, created in collaboration with social workers, spelled out everything from medical needs and mobility goals to communication preferences and behavioral supports. They were more than paperwork; they were the lifelines that kept everyone safe, seen, and cared for.

Joe's role expanded quickly. He coordinated doctor and dental appointments, helped track rising prescription costs, and stayed on top of every resident's evolving needs. As he stepped into administration, his reach only grew, handling state inspections, working closely with maintenance, and making sure every aspect of The Angelus kept running smoothly.

When hurricanes approached, it was Joe who oversaw evacuations. Moving a dozen people—many in wheelchairs or needing medical equipment—was no small feat, but Joe made it look seamless. He also kept our fundraisers going strong and even came up with a few new ones, which you'll read more about later. During staffing shortages and turbulent times, Joe stayed the course, keeping our doors open and our hearts steady.

In time, Joe remarried, and his wife Laura became a true partner, helping with the day-to-day, managing the emotional load, and staying committed to our mission. Together, they navigated the increasing weight of regulations and staffing challenges. No matter what came their way, they made sure The Angelus remained a safe and loving home.

When Joe retired, his daughter Joelle stepped into his role, with Laura by her side. Having worked at The Angelus throughout college and earning her master's in human resources, Joelle was ready. With Joe still nearby for guidance, a third generation took the helm.

Through the dedication of our family and the unwavering support of our community, The Angelus has endured. And now, with Joelle leading, a new chapter begins, one built on the same foundation of care, commitment, and love that Joe helped lay all those years ago.

MARCUS:
A TESTAMENT TO ENDURING SPIRIT

Marcus arrived at The Angelus on the same stormy February day as Caroline. He was a young non-verbal boy, small for his age, every movement a challenge. His muscles tightened involuntarily, often causing him to stiffen and arch in discomfort.

Feeding Marcus was especially challenging. Each time I tried to offer him a spoonful of food, his tongue reflexively pushed it back out. It took patience, and trial and error before I found a way to support him. I sat on the floor with a foam cushion across my lap, gently cradling his body between my legs. It was slow, delicate work, but the trust that formed between us was unmistakable. When he smiled after a successful meal, it felt like a small victory for both of us.

A visiting physical therapist suggested we look into getting a custom-fitted wheelchair for Marcus, saying it would better support his posture. Two weeks later, his new chair, complete with a supportive headrest, lateral supports, and secure safety straps, arrived. That chair changed everything. He could sit upright comfortably for the first time. Mealtime became easier, and he began to seem more at ease in his body.

Marcus had a way of connecting with people, especially the young women on staff. His bright eyes and playful grin made everyone feel special. He especially loved being in the water. Floating in the pool freed him from the tension that gripped him on land. In those weightless moments he beamed with joy.

As time went on, I could see that Marcus needed more consistent nutritional support. A medical device was recommended to ensure he received the nourishment his body required. The results were immediate and wonderful. He grew stronger, gained weight, and shot up several inches in height. Though he never spoke, he didn't need words to express himself. His face could communicate joy, frustration, affection, and humor with astonishing clarity.

One unforgettable weekend, Marcus's family came to visit. It was the first time I met them. His mother, who had been through her own challenges, arrived with other relatives. The house was full of warmth and laughter that day. I watched Marcus soaking in their presence, smiling at the familiar voices and faces. It was the only time they visited, but it was a beautiful, healing reunion.

Today, Marcus is in his fifties. He continues to live in a nurturing environment, supported by caregivers who know and love him. His life is a testament to what's possible when care, dignity, and consistency are given freely. Watching Marcus grow and thrive over the years has been one of the quiet joys of my life. His story reminds me that love doesn't need to be loud to be powerful, and that presence, patience, and belonging can transform a life.

TRAVIS "BEAR":
THE GENTLE ROAR OF RESILIENCE

Travis became part of our group home in 1979, following two other children from North Florida. It was a heartbreaking story that began with the loss of his father, who had been tragically killed. His mother, overwhelmed with grief and the demands of raising three boys on her own, sought help. She was disappointed with the care Travis had received in a state-run setting and, after hearing about us through a social worker reached out in the hopes of finding something better. She visited with Travis's older brother to talk through what kind of support he might need, and it was then that we first heard his affectionate nickname: "Bear."

Travis was seven years old when he came to us, non-verbal, with significant physical limitations, and a personality that glowed through his eyes and smile. He arrived in a wheelchair designed for both feeding and reclining, and although his challenges were many, it was his sweetness, his giggle, and that unmistakable grin that captured my heart and the heart of everyone who met him.

His nickname, "Bear," became clear not long after he settled in. One afternoon, during a rare moment of frustration, he let out a deep, unmistakable roar; a guttural growl that startled me a bit. "Oh my goodness," I said with a patient smile, "you have quite a roar there, Travis. You are a bear?" His furrowed brow began to relax, and then a little smile appeared. Travis adapted quickly to life at The Angelus.

At school and home, he surprised me with how mobile he could be. He would roll himself down the hallway that led to the bedrooms. My daughter Perri, who often spent weekends helping me, shared a special bond with him. On those mornings, Travis would excitedly make his way to the room where Perri stayed, kicking at the door with his feet until she woke up. Of course, she only pretended to be annoyed with Travis kicking at her door and waking her up. He would burst into full-body laughter. I had so much fun listening to their silly and sweet ritual that became part of their story.

Swimming became one of Travis's favorite activities after a generous donation allowed us to build a pool. A volunteer named Bill took Travis swimming every week, often ending the day with a trip to McDonald's for fries and milkshakes. During those car rides, Bill played along, as we all did when Travis's mischievous streak surfaced. When they got home, I would hear stories about things like how Travis changed his mind, sending Bill back through the drive-thru, both laughing the whole time. Bill and the Bear had a genuine bond. Bill made every visit with his pal so much fun and even included his own family on some of their adventures. I will always be grateful to Bill who made Travis feel included and important.

As I got to know Travis, it was clear to me that he understood far more than many assumed. With Elaine's encouragement, he was reassessed at school, and new options opened up. Travis was able to attend a new school, and that's where he was introduced to something pretty remarkable: a communication board that used eye-pointing. It was a complicated setup at first; a large, see-through plastic board with words and symbols printed in squares across the surface was placed on the tray in front of him. His teacher would sit directly across from him, carefully watching where his eyes landed. A simple "yes" might be in the upper right square, while "no" was in the upper left. A picture of a glass of water might be in the lower right corner, and a plate of food in the lower left.

As he got the hang of it, the system became more advanced. More squares were added, and sometimes he had to eye-point to two different locations—say, the second square down in the third column—to communicate something more specific.

It required a lot of concentration and understanding on his part, but he rose to the challenge. Eventually, the whole thing was upgraded to an electronic version that could spell out words, which worked especially well for students who had the ability to spell.

Travis took to it quickly. He was clever and full of surprises. Sometimes, he'd deliberately give the wrong answer just to see the look on your face. That little sparkle of mischief made me proud. His humor, which had always been there, now had a new way to shine through. But not everyone saw it that way. The school decided he was "too immature" to continue using the system, which broke my heart a little, but I understood their point of view.

Travis's family remained a steady part of his life, visiting regularly. When they arrived, the house filled with laughter and joyful screeches. Though he couldn't return home, their love for him—and his for them—was never in question. When it was time to say goodbye, it was always heartbreaking to see Travis's sad face and quivering bottom lip, but he accepted it with grace and waited eagerly for the next visit.

Just like most parents, I was always interested in finding activities for the children outside of school. We didn't have a computer or Google back then; we had friends, teachers, and social workers, a beehive of information. I heard about a therapeutic horseback riding initiative that sounded like just the kind of activity I was looking for. It turned out to be a great experience for Travis, and for a time, he rode with confidence and joy, his helmet askew, a grin stretching across his face as he sat proudly in the saddle. Volunteers walked beside him, offering gentle support, while we cheered from the fence. Something about the rhythm of the ride calmed his body and lifted his spirit. "Look at me!" his eyes seemed to say as he passed by.

Even after he was no longer able to ride, he still wanted to go and watch some of his housemates from the sidelines. I think about the very special community of people involved with that program and the volunteers who made it happen. It was more than a horseback riding experience. There was something really special about seeing the bond between rider, walker, and horse. It just made us happy.

In 1986, Travis moved to Hudson, where he continued to blossom. He completed high school and then participated in the day program we established. And although he missed his good friends Bill and Perri, he made new friends. And by this time, I had lots of help and volunteers to help me find and sometimes create our own activities. Travis wanted to do it all: concerts, wrestling matches, bowling, and fishing trips.

Many years passed, and Travis's health began to decline. He passed away peacefully at home on a summer night in 2006. His family held a funeral in his hometown, where he was laid to rest beside his brother. After 27 years, Travis had become my "Honey Bear." He taught me what quiet courage looks like and how even the gentlest soul can leave the loudest roar in your heart.

CHASE:
A MISCHIEVOUS SPIRIT
WITH AN UNSTOPPABLE WILL

I first learned about Chase through a call from the VA office in another county. They explained that they weren't equipped to care for very young children and that a little boy needed immediate placement. He had already endured more than most kids his age. The relative who had been caring for him, a veteran, had recently passed away, leaving him with no one to turn to. The VA had been working to secure him a wheelchair, but for the time being he was confined to a canvas stroller.

When I met Chase, I saw a little boy, non-verbal and unable to walk, with a spark of mischief and determination. I endearingly called him my little "Huckleberry Finn." He was the fifth child welcomed to our group home that week! And because he didn't yet have the equipment to safely go to school, I spent the first couple of days simply getting to know him. What I discovered amazed me. Chase had the upper body strength of a champion. Though his legs couldn't carry him, his arms were like little engines. He would pull himself across the floor with incredible speed, always heading toward something that fascinated him.

One of his favorite pastimes was investigating the empty wheelchairs lined up in the living room. I kept a watchful eye on his fascination with the wheels. I can still see his gleeful grin as he spun the wheels back and forth, and then, he tipped the whole thing over. He laughed so hard, seemingly very delighted with his accomplishment.

I had an idea for an activity that might help Chase feel more connected to the other kids. We arranged a circle on the carpeted living room floor, using bean bag chairs and low-to-the-ground adaptive floor sitters designed for children who needed extra support. With everyone at the same level, Chase could safely roll around inside the circle, pausing to interact with his friends as he pleased. It created a space where he could be himself, while still feeling part of the group. This seemed to work well for a short time, when Daisy called out loudly, "Colleen, he's 'scaping!" Sure enough, Chase, giggling and excited, found a way out by moving between or over the bean bags and over the kids that were in them. No matter how many times we tried, he always found a way out, and Daisy was always on alert.

For his safety and the safety of the others, we moved him to a room where he could explore freely. That's when I learned another fascinating side of Chase, his joyful determination to rearrange everything within reach, moving his crib and emptying dresser drawers. His laughter filled the house, and we jokingly began to refer to him as our "problem child"—always with affection— and always with a smile.

Two weeks later, Chase's sturdy new wheelchair arrived, and it was a game-changer. He joined the other children at school, where his mischievous curiosity charmed the staff. I was so pleased to know that a special play area was created just for him, and he embraced it with his usual enthusiasm. And then one day, I got a call from the school social worker to tell me that Chase had reached over and tipped another child's wheelchair. Thankfully, there were no injuries. Chase's reaction to the whole thing was hilarious laughter. Well, we all learned a valuable lesson in setting boundaries, with plenty of space between Chase and anyone within reach.

At home, we learned to adapt to his unique spirit. I had the idea of cutting his bedroom door in half, like a stable door, so we could peek in without risking one of his grand escape plans. Chase brought so much energy and laughter into our home. Oh, he was a handful, alright, but I liked his fearless curiosity and unshakable will. He reminded me every day that even the smallest joys can make the biggest difference.

FIRE SPRINKLER:
A COMMUNITY'S GIFT OF PROTECTION

The house was finally complete. I felt so blessed and grateful for what we had accomplished. We built something beautiful and full of life. But before we could all really settle in, a new challenge emerged. Expansion! We welcomed so many new children, and with that growth came an unexpected but critical requirement: installing a fire sprinkler system. Though daunting, it was essential to ensure the safety of the children in our care who couldn't move quickly in an emergency.

I thought back to my school days at St. Paul's and remembered a classmate, Fred Hagan. He was now Lt. Fred Hagan of the St. Petersburg Firefighters Sertoma Club. When I reached out, he didn't hesitate. Our group home was selected as the very first recipient of the new plastic fire extinguisher system; a project that made headlines! Lt. Hagan, along with Captain Britner and the Sertoma Club, led the charge to raise funds for a portion of the project. The remaining costs were covered through generous contributions from several companies, including AAA Fire Protection Equipment of Tampa, Banks Supply in St. Petersburg, Bill Sweet Pump Company in St. Petersburg, and Grinnell Fire Protective Systems in Tampa.

A dedicated team of firefighters and volunteers gave up an entire weekend to install the system. It was no small feat navigating around wheelchairs, working carefully with as little disruption of our household as possible, and meticulously mapping out every inch of the system. Their determination never wavered. When the work was done, they left the house spotless, as if they had never been there, except for the new sprinkler system overhead, quietly standing guard.

What moved me most was what I saw in the firefighters' faces as they packed up to leave. They had come to install a system, but they left with something more. Seeing the children, knowing who they were protecting, gave the work a deeper meaning.

Looking back, I believe it was my childhood schoolmate Fred, or I should say Lt. Hagan, and the Firefighters Sertoma Club example that lit the way. Once they stepped in, others followed. It wasn't just about fire safety; it was about community, about people showing up for children they didn't even know, simply because it was the right thing to do. I had never asked for much, but I was learning that when you lead with heart, others will meet you there. What those people gave us that weekend was more than a fire sprinkler system; they gave us a sense of belonging and a reminder that we weren't in this alone.

MICHAEL AND DAISY:
A BOND THAT ENDURED BEYOND TIME

Michael and Daisy were among the first children to arrive in early 1979, just days after we opened our doors. They were siblings, close in age and spirit, both born with significant physical challenges. Their parents had cared for them with extraordinary love and devotion. But when their father's job required long absences, their mother found herself overwhelmed as the sole caregiver to two children with extensive needs. Her decision to place them in our care was heartbreaking, but it was also brave. She trusted us with something sacred, and we never forgot that.

Michael was eight years old and non-verbal. His calm presence and beaming smile made him a joy to be around. Daisy, his ten-year-old sister, was just as lovable as her brother but in her own unique way. She was verbal and a delightful little chatterbox, rarely seen without a baby doll in her arms, and tenderly feeding her. Unlike Michael, Daisy could feed herself, especially when cookies were involved. But like her brother, she needed full support in most other aspects of her care.

At first, their mother visited daily, teaching us everything she could about how to care for her children, especially their hair and skin. She taught me about oils and explained the importance of regular moisturizing. I was so grateful to learn. Her guidance went beyond routine; it was an expression of deep, culturally rooted love. Over time, as her trust in us grew, her visits became less frequent, but her devotion to her children never wavered.

Michael quickly bonded with my son Marty. They had so much fun together. I remember how much joy Marty brought as he pushed Michael in a toy car around the house. When I think about those delightful days, I can still hear the laughter. Daisy, meanwhile, charmed everyone with her endless imagination. Whether she was baking pretend cakes in Aunt Lou's kitchen or giggling over a game of hide-and-seek with her "love bugs," Daisy's joy was pure and contagious.

I'll never forget the day Daisy surprised everyone at a school meeting. Her teacher's jaw nearly dropped when Daisy turned to me with a big, open-mouthed smile and said, "Hello, Colleen," clear as day. I'm not sure if it was the "P" sound that tripped her up, or if that joyful grin somehow transformed "Pauline" into "Colleen." Either way, it was the sweetest greeting I've ever heard. "Hello Daisy," I said, adding, "Hey, tell me again who all your friends are." The teacher was stunned. She had no idea Daisy could speak, let alone that she knew the names of every classmate. My heart swelled with pride and broke at the same time. How could it be that no one had heard her voice until now?

That moment revealed something quite profound: Daisy had been fully aware all along, quietly, and happily, I might add, absorbing the world around her. It was hard to accept that in all her time at school, she had never been invited to engage, to speak, to be seen for the vibrant child she was. And yet, there she was, confident, knowing, and ready. It was a powerful reminder for me that even the most well-meaning educators can underestimate children when they don't speak or move in expected ways. Assumptions can silence a voice long before a disability ever could. Daisy taught me that lesson.

Just as we prepared to move The Angelus to our new location in Hudson, we faced an unimaginable loss. Michael passed away suddenly. The grief was overwhelming. Daisy, remarkably resilient, never asked about her brother, but her silence spoke louder than words ever could. I can't be sure how much Daisy understood, any more or less than any other child, but it just seemed to me that she carried her brother's presence with her in the subtlest of ways. During meals, she would pause and glance toward his usual seat, as if checking in. She continued her playful routines, letting out a giggle or mimicking his favorite sounds just enough to make us feel he was still nearby. I think it was the bond between Daisy and Michael, between sister and brother, which endured; not in grand gestures, but in the everyday moments that once defined their time together.

The move to Hudson was smooth for Daisy, who adapted with her usual quiet strength. Her family remained a steady presence in her life, visiting for holidays and picnics, their love surrounding her like a favorite blanket. As the years passed, Daisy's health began to decline. Eventually, she was moved to a nursing home closer to her mother and grandmother. During her final months, I visited as often as I could. And even as she grew weaker, her spirit never dimmed.

When Daisy passed away in her forties, her funeral was held in a church filled with music and memory. Draped above the sanctuary was a giant quilt created by her family, each patch bearing a photo or memory and telling the story of Daisy's life; her smile, her sweetness, her spark. The church followed a tradition where only the immediate family walked behind the casket. But then, Daisy's mother turned to me and gently took my hand, inviting me to walk with them. I was speechless. It was a gesture so powerful and so humbling that it brought tears to my eyes. In that moment, I felt the full weight of the bond we had shared, and the depth of trust and love Daisy's family had extended to us.

The time I spent with Michael and Daisy taught me so much. What stays with me most is the unbreakable bond I witnessed between brother and sister, and between parents and their children. Their love was quiet but constant, and it wrapped around all of us. Michael and Daisy will always hold a place in my heart. They became part of my family, and they always will be.

AMBER:
THE HEART THAT BUILT A HOME

Amber's journey is the very reason The Angelus exists. Her story of unimaginable hardship became the catalyst that drove me to navigate a maze of regulations and red tape to create a safe space, determined to make a home where children like her could thrive.

At just nine years old, Amber had already endured more challenges than most face in a lifetime. She was one of several children in a home where her needs often went unmet. Amber's special education teachers noticed when she arrived at school hungry, dirty, and disheveled. One day she was found in the same spot where the school bus had dropped her off the afternoon before. Her small body, confined to a wheelchair, was marked by insect bites.

Alarmed, the school intervened. With no better options available, Amber was placed in a temporary group home for women. Though well-intentioned, the arrangement was far from suitable for a child in a wheelchair. The caretakers of this women's home were not happy about taking care of a child with needs they were not accustomed to dealing with. When they had something to do outside the home, they had to take Amber along because there wasn't enough help. And this is how we all met at a behavior modification course where I was preparing for my new path of opening a group home for troubled kids. Then I met Amber, and the entire direction of my life changed.

Amber's caregivers were not shy about telling me how unhappy they were, saying they were "stuck with this kid," with one of the biggest problems being maneuvering a wheelchair through their split-level home, having to lift it several times a day. I could tell that Amber understood what was being said. I also learned that the only other alternative was even more unsuitable, a mental hospital, an outcome no one could accept.

I couldn't stop thinking about her. She didn't just need shelter; she needed belonging and dignity, a home where she could feel wanted. I worked long, sleepless nights as a medical transcriptionist, deciphering every difficult report, all while raising the funds needed to purchase a larger house and navigating the bureaucratic maze of strict licensing requirements. Throughout the many challenges, Amber stayed in my heart, reminding me what was at stake.

And so here we are at the beginning of a new chapter in Amber's story, just nine years old, moving into her new home, with us, at The Angelus. Non-ambulatory, non-verbal, partially blind, and using only one hand with any control, Amber radiated with life. She had a delightful sense of humor, always catching the joke and following every funny story. Her sharp hearing allowed her to follow conversations around her, even the gentle gossip of the staff, responding with a knowing smile and a hearty laugh.

It wasn't long before I saw what others had missed. Amber had always been aware, always engaged. So, once again, we had one of our kids reassessed. The results placed her in a more appropriate learning environment where she flourished.

Amber quickly became an essential part of our family. She embraced her role as our little "babysitter," always tending the younger residents with great care, often reaching out to hand a toy to a nearby child. Amber trained dozens of staff members, teaching them, through her patience, how to support her during baths, meals, and transfers. Though feeding remained difficult due to her condition, Amber tried. Messes were part of the process, but her persistence never wavered. Sometimes, the teasing of her classmates stung, though she did her best to rise above it.

Amid the challenges, Amber found joy in the simplest things. Music made her happiest, and she adored the recorded stories from Books for the Blind. When she got a little older, she thoroughly enjoyed those young adult teen novels, keeping up with the fast-paced narratives and laughing hysterically over the antics of the young protagonists. She was deeply sensitive, forming strong bonds with those around her, and goodbyes were never easy. Whether someone was leaving at the end of their shift or moving on to another job, she felt it. Every departure left a mark on her heart.

Perhaps the deepest wound in Amber's tender spirit was the loss of Sam, the love of her life. Like Amber, Sam was non-verbal and non-ambulatory, but they found each other in their shared understanding. While some dismissed their relationship as "cute," I knew better. Their love was real. For ten years, they comforted one another in sickness, stayed close at every opportunity, and expressed something profound without ever needing a word. And that sounds like love to me.

Amber's life at The Angelus continued to flourish. She attended Girl Scout camp and participated in school programs that expanded her world. After graduating from high school, she participated in The Angelus Adult Day Training Program and embraced every opportunity to engage with life: going to football games, concerts, wrestling matches, baby showers and birthday parties, fundraising events, and church services. She wanted to be part of everything, and I remember how everything was more fun because of her.

One year, one of Amber's personal support goals was to take a trip to New York City to visit Perri and her daughter, Tori. It was a big dream. One that would take planning, budgeting, and a lot of determination. Together, we sat down and worked through the costs: gas, miles, food, lodging. It was clear it wouldn't be cheap. But Amber was set on going, and I was set on helping her make it happen.

Amber had always enjoyed baking, especially brownies and carrot cake, so we came up with a plan. Every Saturday, we met in the ADT kitchen, and she got to work baking sweet treats to sell. She helped design a little flyer explaining her goal, and soon enough, she was getting regular orders from staff and friends. One of the employees worked at the Social Security office and brought in Amber's brownies. Apparently, they were a hit there, too.

Week after week, Amber cracked the eggs, measured out the dry ingredients, greased the cake pans, and wrapped up each order with care. We used the commercial mixer and ovens, and she never missed a Saturday. Once we hit our goal, I tallied up the money she'd earned from all those brownies and cakes, and we were ready.

I invited my twelve-year-old granddaughter Julie to come with us since she'd never been to New York either. Dave outfitted our large handicapped-accessible van with a custom "changing table" setup, and I carefully mapped out a route that included a motel stop halfway up. I also made sure to pack the Hoyer lift, since Amber had grown too heavy for one person to lift safely.

We were somewhere in Georgia when it hit me. I had forgotten the sling for the lift. My heart dropped. I called Joe, who sprang into action and found a medical supplier in Savannah that carried what we needed. It was a detour, but we made it and got back on the road with a brand-new sling.

That night, at the motel, we hit another snag. Julie was in charge of getting the Hoyer lift into the room, but the bed was too low. The lift wouldn't fit underneath! We were tired, hungry, and more than a little cranky, but Amber burst into laughter, and that was all it took. We sat on the floor, laughing with her. I called down to the front desk, and within minutes, they brought up a cot that worked perfectly.

The next morning, after a good night's sleep and a hearty breakfast, we hit the road again. We made it to Perri's house, where there was a makeshift ramp up the front steps of the house. It worked like a charm. That evening, we gathered around the table and shared a home-cooked meal. Tori and Julie took it upon themselves to be Amber's tour guides, and the three of them stayed up late making plans for sightseeing in the city. We rode the Staten Island Ferry and caught a stunning view of the

Statue of Liberty. We strolled through Central Park, explored the colorful streets of Chinatown, and did our best to keep to the sidewalks, though we quickly learned that not every corner in New York City is built with a wheelchair in mind. Some intersections had no ramps at all, and we had to get creative, sometimes backtracking or relying on a helpful stranger. Still, we felt the energy of the city, the movement, the noise, the hustle and bustle of it all. It was the trip of a lifetime. And Amber had baked her way there.

Thinking back to that adventure, I realize it really was a trip of a lifetime because with all the new regulations in place, a trip like that just wouldn't happen today. Even just a few years after that trip, a former teacher came to visit—someone who had taken Amber on outings when she was young. The joy on Amber's face said everything but by this time, regulations had stopped those one-on-one interactions. Their reunion reminded me just how meaningful those kinds of connections can be. While well-meaning, the new policies strip away the personal bonds. For Amber, those long-lasting bonds meant everything.

Decades later, Amber is in her fifties and still calls The Angelus home. Though she remains a source of joy, there are days when she falls into silence, when grief overwhelms her, when tears come without warning. She carries the loss of the people who knew her best. And today's new staff, though well-intentioned, often don't know her history. They see only her present needs, not the full life that shaped her. When she breaks down, they struggle to understand why.

Amber is the reason The Angelus exists. She is our beginning, and I believe she is still our guide. She is the living reminder that every life, no matter how difficult, how filled with challenges, holds immeasurable value and the power to build a house filled with love.

PETE AND SAM:
A BOND THAT DEFIED THE ODDS

Pete and Sam's story is unique and one of love and the unbreakable bond between brothers. Although fifteen years of their lives were spent apart, their lives remained deeply intertwined, shaped by remarkable challenges and triumphs. Pete's consistent determination to bring his older brother Sam home brought a profound sense of purpose to his life at The Angelus.

Pete arrived at The Angelus in January 1980, after spending his early life at an institutional facility for profoundly disabled children. Diagnosed with severe disabilities, he had lived in a ward where growth opportunities were scarce. Pete spent his days in a large, windowless, sparse room with only a single chair and a clock on the wall. Children lay on mats on the floor, their voices reduced to guttural sounds and occasional screeches, under the watchful eye of a kind staff member named Sophie. It was Sophie who described the emptiness of the room, the absence of stimulation, and the quiet heartbreak of watching children grow up without laughter or learning. Sophie ensured they were safe, clean, and as comfortable as possible, but there were no toys, and no sense of childhood joy.

Yet Pete found meaning and hope in the smallest things. Sophie described how he would stare at the clock, knowing that every Wednesday at 11:00 a.m., Pam, the Phys Ed teacher would arrive. Pam worked with ambulatory children but took an interest in Pete. She noticed his bright eyes and determination as he scooted across the floor using his knees and the tops of his feet. Pam was so impressed that she asked Sophie if she could bring him to her class in the gym. Sophie was delighted and agreed. Make no mistake about it. Pete hatched that plan and followed through with grand tenacity until, every day at 11 a.m., Pete got to escape that room and go to Pam's gym class.

Pete exercised with the other children who were training for the Special Olympics. He began to mimic the exercises and routines. Pete's determination shone through, and very soon, he too was training for the Special Olympics. Over time, he developed his own routine, including forward and backward rolls and a three-point stance. The other students encouraged him by clapping and cheering at his every move. Likewise, Pete was their biggest fan, cheering as they practiced their running and jumping. Pam enrolled him in the Special Olympics competition, doing a log roll event and gymnastics, performing his expanded routine. He was so excited to take the trip to Tampa with his fellow athletes and stay in a student dorm. At the Olympic stadium, Pete's hard work was rewarded. Not only did he land two gold medals in gymnastics, but by interacting with the other Special Olympic athletes, he discovered a wonderful world outside of the world he lived in, a world where children lived in group homes and with families.

Pam told me that before they even got back from the competition, Pete found ways to let Pam know he wanted to live at a group home. With consistency and with great urgency, he kept telling her every time he saw her, even trying to say the words "group home" with two-syllable grunting sounds. By answering Pam's yes/no questions by holding up three fingers for "yes" and two fingers for "no," she was able to understand what he was trying to tell her. Pam's advocacy led to Pete being placed on a list for group home placement. The following year, his file reached The Angelus. I agreed to have Pete come for a week on a trial basis. And when Pete arrived with his caregiver, Sophie, on that fateful day in January, he immediately got to work impressing everyone; he smiled, kneeled on the carpeted floor, clapped his hands twice, and proceeded to demonstrate his Special Olympics routine. This was also the day that Sophie explained as much as she could about Pete and expressed how pleased she was that Pete had a chance to live in a group home of eight, compared to the forty he was currently living with.

When reading his file, we learned that he had an older sister and an older brother. Both boys were born with severe physical challenges, while their sister was able-bodied. In those days, babies who could not hold their heads up or communicate were classified as "imbeciles" or "idiots." Their mother was told her boys would not live very long, and she was encouraged to place them in an institution. The family tried to care for the boys at home, but the emotional and financial toll became too difficult, especially while running a growing business. The brothers were placed in separate wards in a state facility at ages three and five. The family visited them just a few times before stopping and ending all communication.

Years later, we met their sister Debbie, and she told us how upset she was when her brothers left home. She went on to explain that going to the state facility for visits was too stressful, as the boys cried when they left. "Mom decided to never go back to visit them again," she said. And they never did. That day was the last time the boys saw their sister. She never came back either.

Pete adapted very well to his new environment at The Angelus. He quickly learned how to use the remote control for the TV and enjoyed searching for cartoon and wrestling shows. He loved kneeling on the floor and leafing through the Sears Christmas catalog, where he found cowboy boots. He got my attention, constantly, persistently, signaling to himself and then pointing to the cowboy boots. I understood what he was telling me, but his feet were completely twisted around. He couldn't wear shoes, let alone cowboy boots. He could only wear knit booties that kept his feet warm. I responded to him in an acknowledging kind of way, "Those are cool boots, huh, Pete?" He would put up his three-finger sign for "yes" with complete determination. Maybe I was thinking he would eventually find something else in that catalog to get excited about, but he never did.

As it happened, he had a scheduled orthopedic appointment. During that visit, Pete signaled with his feet and looked at me as if to say, "Ask the doctor about how his feet could be fixed, so that he could wear cowboy boots." So, I did just that. "Would it be possible?" The doctor described a procedure: "We would have to do a little carpentry to adjust the shape of the foot." And Pete, listening intently, spark in his eyes, rocking back and forth, held up his three fingers, "YES!"

We were at a teaching hospital, and that made a difference. The doctor, along with a group of interns, saw the case not just as a request for boots, but as a rare and valuable opportunity. The structural challenges in Pete's feet offered a real-time lesson in bone fusion and function. What might not have been considered medically necessary in another setting became a teaching moment for future orthopedic specialists. And for Pete, it was a turning point. His dream wasn't silly at all; it was the start of something real.

Pete never complained during the long, painful recovery after each foot reconstruction surgery three months apart. Assured that wearing cowboy boots was indeed going to be possible, I bought them for him and placed them on the hospital bedside table to hold and look at while he was healing. The day came, and finally, he was able to put on his cowboy boots. Pete walked around the house with a walker and the biggest smile I had ever seen. In school, he was appointed bathroom leader, where he proudly led a line of boys to the restroom. And that's how Pete gets things done. With persistence, patience, and never giving up.

Pete was continuing his Special Olympics training at his new school when I was recruited by the P.E. teacher to chaperone a group of boys at the next event. I assisted in the dorm, cafeteria, and at the event itself. And for the record, Pete won even more medals that day, but this time, he was competing in the Walking Events!

The only other problem Pete had was eating. He had a severe swallowing disorder that caused him to cough and sputter, often sending food onto whoever was feeding him. No matter how thin we made the puréed food, his uncontrollable coughing persisted, and at fourteen years old, he weighed only thirty-six pounds, far too little for a boy his age. Determined to help, my son Joe who was a student at airplane mechanic school, devised creative strategies to encourage Pete to eat. He created a daily chart, grading Pete's eating habits, and offered a small monetary reward of twenty-five cents for good progress. Money was an excellent motivator for Pete. He loved it so much that he would emerge from his bedroom, hopping and holding his piggy bank, when visitors would stop by. As he approached our guests with his signature smile and sparkle, he would start shaking it, delighted to share the sounds of the coins inside. I had to explain to him that asking guests for money was not proper manners, but shaking his piggy bank in his room to hear the coins he earned from Joe was perfectly fine!

Still, swallowing remained challenging for Pete, and progress was slow. So, Joe struck a deal with him. If Pete reached fifty pounds, he would take him on an airplane ride. Motivated by this goal, Pete slowly gained weight, eventually reaching forty-five pounds. Not quite fifty pounds, but as promised, Joe arranged the flight with his instructor, since he was graduating that week and his wedding to Elaine was just around the corner.

The day Pete finally went up in the small plane was unforgettable. To celebrate, we spread large sheets on the front lawn, forming his initials. When the plane flew over, the instructor tipped the wings in greeting as we waved and cheered from below. It was a joyful day for all of us.

Although eating remained a struggle, I believe those efforts—the deal, the goal, the progress—meant something deeper. It gave Pete pride. Eventually, Pete needed a more reliable way to get his nourishment. In 1982, he was fitted with a gastrostomy tube that allowed him to receive the nutrition his body needed, safely and consistently. From there, he grew stronger every day.

Every morning, when I would go in to feed Pete his formula, he would say "Sam." First thing in the morning, while he was relaxed, he could form a few words, but as he awakened, his neck muscles would tighten, and he could not form words anymore. He could answer yes and no questions using three fingers for "yes" and two fingers for "no," so we were able to hold long, meaningful conversations in the morning during his feeding. He constantly wanted to talk about Sam. Pete knew Sam's birthday was in August, and he wanted to go and visit his brother to bring him a gift with the money he earned from Joe during his feeding sessions. I suggested a small portable radio, and he thought that was a great idea. We planned a trip to the state facility. Pete was so excited all during the trip, tapping his feet to the beat of music on the radio.

When we arrived, Pete decided he wanted to walk in, and of course, he was wearing cowboy boots. He stood straight and tall as he walked using his walker, and he ignored all the staff who remembered him and were amazed at his progress. When we got to Sam's ward, there he was, strapped in a wheelchair. Pete just fell on him with hugs. It was very emotional, and we were all so happy to see the boys together. Pete and Sam have their own form of communication, and it was obvious to all of us that they were talking about "home." Once again, I explained to Pete that Sam could not leave the hospital setting, and I could not take care of him because he needed doctors and nurses. He had heard this from me several times, but he still persisted in saying that I could take care of him. I told Pete that we would come more often to visit.

Sam's gentle nature endeared him to the staff, particularly Momma Van, who cared for him deeply. She occasionally took him to her home during the day and even cared for his pet turtles. Sam's life was confined to his crib in the infirmary, yet his quiet strength and presence left an impression on everyone who met him.

On our next visit, Pete and I got permission from the nurse to take Sam with us to the beach. We went to a motel, and the boys spent the afternoon watching wrestling on TV and eating Fruit Loops, one piece at a time. I told Sam how Pete got his meals, how we helped him take in all the nutrition he needed, just in a different way than most. When dinnertime came, Sam watched closely as we prepared everything and got Pete settled. Pete just smiled and patted his belly, letting us know it hit the spot.

When we got back to Sam's ward, I surprisingly got permission to take Sam home for a weekend visit for Christmas!! We were so excited and got the house ready for our weekend guest.

What a great Christmas it was! The boys hopped around the house together, watched wrestling on TV, and pretended to wrestle in the living room. They opened gifts together and spread torn wrapping paper all over the living room to the delight of all our other "kids." We were thrilled to see and hear the joy from the brothers, but I was a bit apprehensive when it came time to feed Sam.

He sat in the stroller with his head twisted to one side as I carefully spooned thin oatmeal with brown sugar and cream. He coughed a little but was making a big effort to keep his head up and aligned. He was offered a thick milkshake, which worked better, and he seemed satisfied with his meal. That evening, some of our friends came over to meet Sam, and he did a lot of smiling. He was happy, and he slept well that night. I slept well too, feeling confident that if Sam had a feeding tube, there would be no problem taking care of him. It was so clear to me that the boys had to be together. The next day was bittersweet as we took Sam back. It was hard for Sam not to cry. I could feel Pete's determination bubbling up inside me.

The following week, I talked to our attorney in St. Petersburg, who was also on our Board of Directors. He asked me if Sam had been declared incompetent, and I told him he had not. Because Sam was twenty-two years old, I could legally ask him if he wanted to live with me, and if he said yes, I could take him out!

Exactly four years after Pete came to The Angelus, I drove to that state facility with a stroller, a set of clothes, and a gait belt to use as a safety strap. My heart was racing as I walked in through the front door, and for some reason, there was no one at the front desk!! I felt God was with me, and I went down to the ward that I knew. Sam's crib was close to the door, and he was quietly lying there while some other patient was making loud noises across the large room. Sam saw me, and I indicated to him to be quiet. I whispered to him, "Do you want to come home with me?" and he nodded his head and showed me three fingers, the sign for "yes."

I quickly changed his clothes, put him in the stroller with the gait belt around him, and we went right down the hallway and out the front door. I was almost running at this point, and Sam was quiet with only a few guttural sounds. We got in the van without running the lift, closed the door, and off we went. Once outside the gates, I let out a big sigh of relief and told Sam that I was taking him to The Angelus. Pete was not told because I wasn't really sure this would happen, and I still couldn't believe that it really happened. We had a happy song-filled ride home. Of course, we got a phone call telling us to bring Sam back, but I just referred them to the attorney! We never had any repercussions from the event. Our local newspaper wrote a heartwarming article about this wonderful reunion.

The boys were thrilled. The staff and children all welcomed Sam back, fulfilling Pete's mission. Their reunion brought joy to everyone, enriching our community. Pete and Sam were not only together; they were also part of a big, loving family, and The Angelus was their forever home. As time went on, they participated in the annual Christmas Pageant in Hudson, with Pete conducting the choir of angels and Sam playing the role of a shepherd boy following the star to Bethlehem. They did wheelchair square dances at our annual picnic, which was a celebration and a big thank you for the community's support. Even Momma Van came to visit the boys, and she brought Sam's turtles to be released into Lake Little John with ID markings on their shells.

Over the years, the boys shared many adventures. They went to football games and, of course, got to see a few live wrestling matches! Dave and I took the boys to Washington, D.C., with the help of our dedicated staff member, Ginny. We met our State Representative, toured the White House, and visited the US Treasury, where we received a souvenir sheet of $1.00 bills. The boys were so excited when they saw the statue of Abraham Lincoln sitting in a huge chair, and they were thrilled to take a ride on a subway. On another occasion, we took Pete and Sam to the mountains of North Carolina to visit our friends, the McLaughlin family.

Pete and Sam had the care and security in the way a family does it best. And when it came to supporting their interests, we all had fun sharing in their curiosity and joy. Pete enjoyed working with an equine therapist to learn how to train and walk our miniature horse, and was invited to perform at a miniature horse exhibition in Kentucky. Dave and I took off on another road trip to watch Pete, wearing a huge cowboy hat and his beloved cowboy boots, proudly showing a cheering audience his skills working with a miniature horse. On the way home, we stopped to visit Charlie and Hazel Daniels, yes, that Charlie Daniels, in their beautiful home in Mt. Juliet, Tennessee. Pete loved music and playing the drums. He was encouraged to practice for when our favorite local band played at the fundraiser events. He got pretty good at it and even got to play drum solos with the Embry Brothers Band, while Sam vocalized the song lyrics, singing along with Jesse, the band's lead singer. What fun they all had and what joy they brought to all of us!

Pete had heard about the Mall of America in Minnesota. Joe was able to get us standby tickets. It was wintertime when Pete and I flew North. He was eager to experience snow for the first time and delighted in stepping onto frozen puddles, fascinated by the ice beneath his feet. The mall itself was an adventure, but the highlight for Pete—and sheer terror for me—was the roller coaster suspended near the ceiling. From the ground, it didn't seem so high, but once we ascended, the drop was daunting. Seated between my legs in a log-shaped car, Pete reveled in every thrilling moment, while I was utterly petrified. Afterward, he wanted to ride again, but I had reached my limit.

Sam enjoyed visiting friends, people that he had grown to love and care about. One trip was with one of his favorites, Michelle, who worked at The Angelus when it was in St. Pete. Sam and Michelle had a special bond and got to spend time with her at her beach house. Another trip took Sam to Houston to visit Joe and his family, Elaine, and Joelle. The airplane journey itself was an adventure! He was in awe of the massive aircraft up close and got to peek into the pilot's cabin!

Sam's health eventually declined, and he passed away at fifty-two. Losing him was heartbreaking for all of us, but especially for Pete. The bond they shared ran deep, and though Pete grieved, he carried his brother's spirit with him every single day. He kept spreading that special kind of joy only he could. Pete stayed with us until he was fifty-eight, and even now, I still feel the warmth of their presence. Their journey from separation to reunion, from silence to laughter, was one of the greatest gifts I witnessed at The Angelus. It taught me that love, when nurtured, can bridge any distance. And that hope, even when tested, can endure.

DARIUS:
A BRIGHT SMILE,
A BRIEF STAY, A LASTING LESSON

Darius arrived at The Angelus in the spring of 1979, bringing with him a radiant smile and a cheerful spirit. At ten years old, he was ambulatory but relied on heavy leg braces for mobility. Despite his physical challenges, his happiness was infectious, and his warm presence left an immediate impression on everyone who met him. His adoptive mother, a hardworking single parent, visited every weekend. Her deep love and unwavering dedication to her son were evident.

Though non-verbal, Darius had a gift for communicating through gestures and sounds. He was expressive, aware, and always found a way to make his feelings known. For example, he would take my hand and pull me to the thing or to the place he was talking about. Each day he rode a specially equipped bus to school, secured with a body harness for safety. His joyful spirit made him a favorite among classmates and teachers alike.

Darius's time with us was brief, just four months, but the lessons he left behind were lasting. After school, the children were assisted out of their wheelchairs and gathered on the floor to stretch out and unwind. We had comfy bean bags and specially designed floor seats to help with positioning and comfort. Darius, unlike all of the other children, was able to walk. The challenge we faced was his leg braces. Sometimes his movements were unsteady, and he would lose his balance and tumble unintentionally onto the other children, startling them, his metal braces occasionally causing injuries. To keep everyone safe, I thought it would be a good idea to remove his braces when he came home. But this decision had an unintended impact. Without the braces, Darius returned to crawling, a heartbreaking step backward for a child who had fought so hard to stand tall.

This weighed heavily on me, and after much reflection and with a heavy heart, I had to face the fact that The Angelus was not the best fit for Darius's needs. He required an environment where he could move freely, without the risk of harm to himself or others. I was relieved to learn that Darius was doing great in his new home, a place where he could run and play with children whose physical needs aligned more closely with his own. His devoted mother remained actively involved, ensuring he continued to thrive.

When Darius returned for a visit, we were overjoyed to see him happy and thriving. Watching him run and play with his new friends, his joy and freedom on full display confirmed that the difficult decision we had made was the right one.

Darius's brief stay opened my eyes in a new way, and it became clear: The Angelus needed to focus on non-ambulatory children. It wasn't a shift in mission. It was a deepening of it. Darius reminded me that giving the best care sometimes means knowing when we're not the best fit. And for that, I'll always be grateful.

EMILY:
A SPARK OF JOY
THAT INSPIRED GROWTH

Emily joined The Angelus as a beautiful six-year-old child, her long blonde hair often tied back in a ponytail that she loved to toss playfully. Emily was blind, non-ambulatory, and non-verbal, yet her presence radiated joy and curiosity. She could sit upright for long stretches, unsupported on a blanket, giggling loudly and making chirping sounds as she flipped her ponytail back and forth across her face. The other children were fascinated by her animated movements and often laughed along with her.

Emily's parents lived locally and were attentive to her needs. They carefully monitored her care and brought a substance from a holistic store, derived from seaweed, which they hoped would improve her vision. Though we followed strict guidelines that didn't permit such treatments, their dedication to her well-being was clear.

At school and home, Emily thrived within her abilities. She was fitted with a stander, which helped her strengthen her legs and allowed her to experience a new perspective. During her time with us, Emily's parents were working through some life changes, and when they moved to Pasco County, Emily was able to transition back home. I understood deeply that sometimes families just need time, and I hoped we would always be ready to offer interim care, never with judgment, always with love.

Emily's time with us may have been brief, but it opened my heart to something I hadn't fully seen before. There were so many families like hers doing their best, but needing a place to turn, even if only for a while. Her story reminded me that The Angelus wasn't just a permanent home for some; it could also be a soft place to land during life's harder seasons. By then, we were reaching capacity, and I found myself dreaming of what it might mean to grow. Expansion wasn't just about adding space; it was about meeting the needs we hadn't yet imagined. And Emily helped me see that clearly.

MARA:
A GENTLE SPIRIT, ANCHORED BY LOVE

Mara came to us during a time of crisis. Her family had been holding things together with hope and exhaustion, but something eventually gave way. Her mother, struggling under the strain of raising three daughters while her husband served overseas, left without warning. One day, she was simply gone. The suddenness of her absence sent shockwaves through their fragile world.

At just thirteen, Mara needed full-time care. She was non-verbal, non-ambulatory, and relied entirely on others for feeding, lifting, and bathing; things that required both strength and steadiness. That responsibility fell to her sixteen-year-old sister, Lisa, who stepped in as best she could. But she was still just a child herself, doing the impossible in silence, with no backup and no relief. Their eldest sister had already drifted out of the picture the year before. And now, with their mother gone, Lisa was the only one left.

It didn't take long before the outside world took notice. Concerned neighbors reached out to child protective services. Lisa panicked, terrified of being placed into foster care. She made a desperate decision and fled with her boyfriend, leaving Mara behind.

And that's how Mara came to us - alone, vulnerable, and in urgent need of the kind of love and care that had been missing from her young life. When Mara arrived at The Angelus, her bright blue eyes and soft blonde hair reflected her gentle nature. Non-ambulatory and non-verbal, she adapted well to her new home. She communicated through head gestures and soft sounds, answering yes-or-no questions with ease. Her laughter was infectious, bringing warmth to everyone around her.

Lisa found a way to visit Mara within the first week at the Angelus, assuring us she would return whenever possible to check on her sister. She shared insights into Mara's world, telling us about her love for macaroni and cheese, kittens, and the small stuffed animal she carried to school. Lisa's devotion was evident, and even when she couldn't visit, she called to speak with Mara, knowing her sister could respond in her own way.

Mara's early days at the Angelus were filled with quiet surprises. After all she had endured, no one expected her to be so cheerful. She sat tall in her wheelchair, always smiling when greeting people. When strangers approached, she locked eyes with them, her expression open and joyful. She couldn't speak, but her face was expressive, and her eyes sparkled. How could she appear so light-hearted after such a traumatic separation from her sister? We tried not to assume too much. Maybe it was gratitude. Maybe it was the relief of being safe and cared for. Or maybe it was just Mara—someone whose emotional weather didn't follow obvious rules.

She became a quiet ambassador for the Angelus. On Sundays, Mara went to church with me, and people were drawn to her almost immediately. Her beauty, warmth, and cheerful disposition had a way of drawing people in. Churchgoers started asking about our work at the Angelus. Mara didn't have to say a word. She communicated something essential just by being there.

Once Mara was safely placed at The Angelus, Health and Rehabilitative Services (HRS) contacted her father, a high-ranking military officer stationed overseas. He was shocked to learn that his daughters had been abandoned. His wife had kept their struggles hidden from him. Lisa, now pregnant, had a quick wedding at a small park ceremony. Mara was her maid of honor. Their father returned to duty in Saudi Arabia but kept in touch, sending beautiful gifts for Christmas and birthdays. Mara never saw her mother again, but if she grieved that loss, we never saw a sign. Instead, she found joy in visits from Lisa, especially when her niece came along. Her face lit up, and her hands would reach out gently, curiously.

Mara attended school alongside the other Angelus children, riding the school bus and later graduating from Hudson before transitioning into our adult day program. Her grandmother in north Florida visited when she could, and as she aged, I would take Mara on day trips to her, and to enjoy nice lunches together. The moments with her grandmother were priceless to Mara. The delight she expressed on those days was unmistakable.

Time brought changes we did not expect.

As she grew older, Mara's cheerful disposition slowly began to shift. She became stubborn at times, and, inexplicably, she developed a strong aversion to the color yellow. If a staff member wore anything yellow, Mara would scream, break out in hives, and refuse care. Sometimes she would lash out physically, fighting or biting the person trying to help her. No one could determine the source of her fear. The cause of this extreme reaction was unknown, but it became a serious behavioral issue. Psychiatric evaluations offered little help because Mara couldn't talk or provide any kind of explanation.

These mental struggles took a toll on her physical health. At times, Mara couldn't swallow food, requiring multiple trips to the hospital for treatments. Her needs became more complex than what we could safely manage. There came a point when she needed to be transferred to a facility licensed to manage behavioral challenges.

Strangely, Mara never displayed these behaviors in front of me. She stayed calm in my presence. I found I could manage her easily, but I couldn't always be there. By this time, the Angelus had moved to the country where we had several homes on one large piece of property. Determined to maintain our bond, I visited her on weekends and brought her back to The Angelus for special visits, especially when Charlie Daniels came to perform, as Mara loved seeing him. These short visits were therapeutic. She stayed overnight at the lodge, one of our homes set up for respite care. This privilege became an important part of her behavioral management plan. I continued to attend all her support–plan meetings, advocating for her and ensuring she had the best care possible.

In time, Mara's father retired from the military and remarried. His new wife quickly became a devoted presence in Mara's life, attending her support plan meetings, visiting on weekends, and even taking her to church. It was a turning point, and a natural moment for me to begin stepping back. After so many years, Mara was surrounded by family again: her father, her stepmother, Lisa, and Lisa's children. They showed up. They loved her. And I knew she was finally where she belonged.

Mara's story was never simple. She could not be summed up in easy words or neat conclusions. She challenged us, surprised us, and reminded us that people are rarely just one thing. Through each chapter of her life, she revealed herself in unexpected ways: in glances, in gestures, in the quiet spaces between our hopes and her truth.

She also revealed something to me: that we, at The Angelus, had to continue evolving. Mara's behavioral needs pushed us to think beyond what we had built to imagine care not only as a place of comfort, but as a structure flexible enough to meet people where they are, especially when they can't tell us why they're struggling. Mara helped me see that expansion wasn't just about growing bigger, it was about growing wiser.

She left a permanent mark on all of us, not because she endured, but because she was wholly, wonderfully herself, complex, radiant, and unforgettable.

BEN:
THE LAUGHING ANGEL
WHO TAUGHT US LOVE

Ben came to The Angelus as an emergency placement at just four years old. His father was a long-haul truck driver, often away for weeks at a time. His mother, overwhelmed by the intensity of Ben's care, had left him in the hands of his grandfather. But as Ben's grand mal seizures escalated—sometimes up to ten a day —and his feeding challenges worsened due to a strong tongue thrust reflex, his grandfather could no longer manage on his own. That's when Ben was brought to us.

In those early days, Ben would only eat chocolate pudding. Any attempt to feed him something different would lead to tears and sometimes seizures, so we met him where he was. Slowly, and with patience, we began mixing other soft foods into his pudding, foods like sweet potatoes, applesauce, and mashed carrots, adding one spoonful at a time. He began to accept these new tastes, and as his nutrition improved, so did his sleep and overall comfort. His seizures became less frequent, and a softness began to settle over him. The staff lovingly nicknamed him "Boo," a nod to the little happy sounds he was now making with reduced distress. His personality began to shine.

Ben's thin blond hair grew into soft curls. His whole face changed, his cheeks filled out, and his eyes began to sparkle when someone entered the room. He became known as our "laughing angel," erupting into bright, contagious giggles, especially while being moved back and forth on the swing. What began as pure joy was also having therapeutic benefits, helping him build balance and strength, and supporting the physical therapy he was receiving. Even activities like touching different fabrics or playing with warm and cool objects helped him develop confidence in his body and curiosity about the world.

In time, Ben's seizures were reduced to about once a week. He underwent surgery to remove a vestibular schwannoma, a benign tumor on the nerve that connects the ear to the brain. The tumor had been contributing to his seizures. Ben recovered from the procedure well, and while the surgery didn't restore speech or mobility, it brought him relief.

Though Ben never stood or spoke, he expressed himself clearly through his eyes, laughter, a gift that made people feel happy. His father continued to visit during holidays, often arriving with a quiet gentleness that revealed the deep bond between them. Even after Ben passed away peacefully in his sleep at age twenty-one, his father returned each year to attend The Angelus Christmas pageant in his memory.

Ben didn't live a long life by most measures, but he lived a deeply meaningful one. In the laughter he gave so freely, in the milestones that came not in words or steps but in comfort, joy, and connection, Ben taught us all what care really looks like. He reminded us that presence matters more than perfection, and that no act of kindness, no matter how small, is ever wasted.

DONALD AND ELLY:
THE STRENGTH OF A FAMILY'S LOVE

I first met Donald when a caseworker reached out in urgent need of help. He was just a toddler then, blind and experiencing frequent physical distress. His parents, both living with intellectual disabilities, had been doing everything they could to care for him. They had moved to Florida from North Carolina, hoping the warmer climate might ease some of his medical challenges. His mother stayed home while his father worked a steady job, but the demands of caregiving had become too great, especially after she became pregnant again. That's when the social worker suggested Donald come to stay with us, just for a little while, so the family could catch their breath.

Donald arrived as a blind, non-ambulatory three-year-old with a head full of curly light brown hair and a sweet smile. He giggled when spoken to, a sound that warmed all our hearts. He continued his medication and began receiving therapy through a specialized school program. Every Sunday, his father visited. He would talk to Donald constantly, gently push him in his new wheelchair, and beam with pride. I could see how deeply he loved his son.

He kept us updated on his wife's pregnancy, and when their baby girl, Elly, was born, he was overjoyed. Not long after, the family came to visit Donald so he could meet his new sister. They lived about five miles from The Angelus and had walked the entire way in the sweltering Florida heat, pushing a stroller the whole way. When they arrived, flushed and exhausted, we gave them water and tried to help them cool down. It was then that I realized they didn't own a car. Every visit, every clinic appointment— everything—required that same long walk.

I looked at the baby and saw signs I recognized; the same subtle lack of eye focus, the same uncoordinated, jerky movements I had seen in Donald when he first arrived. Elly didn't respond to movement or light the way a newborn typically might. My heart sank. I couldn't be certain, but I had a strong sense that Elly, too, was blind.

The family continued to visit, but eventually with Elly's growing medical needs and the distance too difficult to manage, the social workers convinced the parents that it was best for Elly to join her brother at The Angelus. Trusting us completely, they agreed, and the siblings were together.

When we later moved to Hudson, regular visits became impossible, a painful reality for the family. Social workers worked diligently to find a placement closer to their homes. During that time, I learned there were relatives in another state who wanted to help. I spoke with a teenage cousin who was full of hope and determination and eager to lend a hand. She was living in difficult circumstances, but her heart was wide open. I spoke with her family, and together we arranged for her to travel to Florida for the summer to be with her cousins while plans for a new placement were still in the works.

She arrived bright-eyed and full of energy. I had printed a little schedule for her, and she dove right in. One of our staff members generously offered her a place to stay and brought her along each morning. She quickly became part of our daily rhythm, helping with morning routines, gently assisting during meals, and learning how to support the children with tenderness and care. It wasn't long before the staff began to trust her with more responsibility. In the afternoon, she joined us for pool time, proudly wearing the new bathing suit our team had picked out for her as a gift.

We gave her a small paycheck for her time, just enough for her to buy a ticket to Disney World. It was a summer none of us would forget. She brought so much light, and when it was time for her to return home, we felt the absence deeply. Though we never heard from her again, the memory of her kindness and the love she gave her cousins remains with me to this day.

Eventually, a placement for Donald and Elly was found closer to their parents. Social workers taught them how to navigate the local bus system so they could visit. A few years later, I learned that Donald had passed away. The parents chose to bring Elly home.

I don't know the details surrounding these events—HIPAA rules protect their privacy—but I did see Elly again. I was at a clinic with one of our residents when I noticed a man gently lifting a girl onto the exam table. It was Elly and her father. She was a giggling and smiling teenager, and he looked at her with the same tenderness I remembered from all those years ago, lovingly wiping her mouth, and whispering softly to her.

That moment stays with me. It was a powerful reminder that people with mental challenges are not lacking in love. Quite the opposite. Donald and Elly's parents faced challenges many of us will never understand, but their devotion was fierce and unwavering. With the right support, their lives, and the lives they touched were rich with meaning, filled with connection, and overflowing with love.

ROSE:
A JOURNEY OF GRACE
THROUGH CHANGE

Rose arrived at The Angelus in the summer of 1980 under heartbreaking circumstances as an emergency placement. Blind, nonverbal, and needing leg braces to assist her mobility, she had always been cared for by her special education teacher. When Rose stopped attending school without explanation, concern quickly grew. By the third day, Rose's compassionate teacher went to Rose's home, where she found the house empty and Rose lying alone on the floor. Thankfully, she was unharmed, but the neglect was undeniable. Authorities intervened, and Rose was brought to The Angelus.

When her parents were located, it became clear that a family crisis had unfolded. Between the difficult parental separation and the care of multiple children, Rose was unintentionally and tragically left behind.

I welcomed Rose to our home, the priority being her well-being. First things first, a warm bath. Removing her leg braces revealed a horrifying discovery. Roaches had taken up residence in the cotton padding. Her wheelchair, too, was infested, with insects emerging from its tubing. We took swift action, treating and cleaning every wheelchair and arranging for professional extermination of the entire home. Despite this troubling start, we were determined to provide Rose with the care and love she deserved. Her father and siblings visited to be sure she was in a good place, but we never saw her mother.

In the weeks that followed, Rose began to blossom. At school, her teachers were thrilled to see her return to class in clean clothes and her hair cut and styled. While initially believed to be completely blind, I noticed subtle behaviors like pulling at the corners of her eyes. This hinted that she might have some vision. An eye examination confirmed that she had partial sight, and with glasses, her world opened up. Though they took some getting used to and she often removed them, Rose learned to wheel herself around, navigating hallways, occasionally bumping into walls and doors. Her determination was inspiring.

Rose's love for food was unmatched, and she approached every meal with gusto. To help her slow down a bit, I gave her a smaller spoon, and she adjusted quickly. I learned that she enjoyed solving wooden puzzles and became quite skilled at it. While television held little appeal, Rose adored the pool. Floating in the water brought her pure joy, and it became one of her favorite activities.

What set Rose apart most was her incredible ability to connect with others. Though she couldn't speak, she communicated warmth with every smile, greeting staff and visitors with the biggest, most genuine hugs. Her affectionate nature made her a beloved member of our family.

Family played a meaningful role in Rose's life. Her grandmother, who lived several miles away, never missed a Christmas Pageant or annual picnic. After more than twenty years, Rose's siblings, now grown with families of their own, came to visit. The reunion was deeply emotional. The moment Rose heard their voices, she lit up with recognition, and there wasn't a dry eye in the room. One of my most treasured memories was attending her grandmother's seventy-fifth birthday celebration at their church. Rose was surrounded by love, beaming with happiness, and it was clear just how much that day meant to her. Her grandmother passed away the following year, but the family's gratitude for the care Rose received stayed with us; a lasting reminder of the connection we had built together.

As of 2025, Rose continues to live a fulfilling life at The Angelus. She still greets visitors with her signature hugs and navigates the hallways in her wheelchair with the same spirited determination. Her love of food, puzzles, and floating peacefully in the pool continues to bring her joy. And as I think about Rose, I am reminded how it all started. What began in crisis has grown into a life filled with comfort, connection, and unmistakable personality.

JAMAL:
A JOURNEY OF HEALING AND JOY

Jamal came to The Angelus on New Year's Eve in 1980 under devastating circumstances. Just a baby, he had recently been discharged from the hospital after suffering severe burns caused by abuse. His injuries were extensive and required significant medical treatment. In the weeks that followed, Jamal developed muscle spasms, causing extreme stiffness, his hands tightly clenching and his legs bending rigidly at the knees. Once Child Protective Services became involved, he was placed with us as an emergency intake.

When he arrived, Jamal's body was tense and still. He found comfort in being held close, but with many children in our care it wasn't always possible to give him one-on-one attention. One afternoon, I placed him next to Michael, another child in our home who was sitting comfortably in a bean bag chair. Michael, though non-verbal, gently wrapped an arm around Jamal. It was a quiet gesture, but a meaningful one. One that I didn't miss. I saw something in that small moment, a flicker of possibility, and from that day forward, we all made sure to seat Jamal next to Michael whenever we could.

At first, Jamal remained tense, unsure of the touch or the boy beside him. But Michael's calm presence never wavered. Again and again, he offered that same gentle gesture, no pressure, no urgency, just quiet reassurance. Michael's calm and consistent presence helped Jamal relax. His shoulders began to soften. His eyes began to search for Michael when he entered the room. In time, he started to smile. And one day he laughed. It came out bright and unexpected, like a sound that had been waiting inside him all along. From that moment on, Jamal's laughter became one of the most joyful sounds in the house.

Jamal required attentive, patient care. His clenched hands needed to be gently opened to clean them. Eventually, he underwent surgery to ease the tightness in his fingers. He was easy to feed, quick to laugh, and seemed happiest when Michael was nearby. Their bond was special, a connection that didn't rely on words; it was something everyone felt.

A few years later, an attorney visited The Angelus to gather information related to a legal case concerning his earlier hospitalization. While the proceedings unfolded, our focus remained on Jamal's well-being and growth, and though the case did not result in a large financial outcome, a portion of the settlement was allocated to cover his past medical expenses through the state system.

Jamal thrived during his years at The Angelus. His spirit was unmistakably full of warmth, playfulness, and affection. He was deeply loved, not only for the joy he brought to everyday life, but for the quiet way he helped people come together. As time passed, however, his health began to decline. With the progression of his breathing difficulties, Jamal's care needs grew beyond what we could safely provide. It was an incredibly difficult decision, but one made with his best interest at heart. After twenty years in our care, Jamal transitioned to a specialized facility where he could receive the advanced care he deserved. Saying goodbye to him was painful and one of the hardest things I ever did, but it was the right thing to do for Jamal. His laughter still echoes in my memory, as does the special bond between two children. I learned that healing doesn't always come from medicine alone. Sometimes, it comes from being seen, being loved, and being held, just as you are.

Holy Name Elementary Undefeated Girls Basketball Team P. E. Teacher
& Coach Pauline Neri (left), 1973

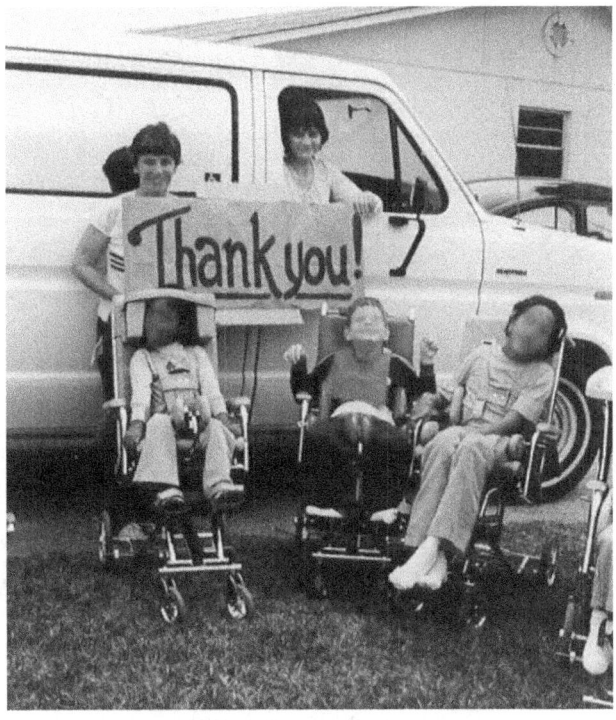

Thank you for the donated van! St. Petersburg, FL
The early years of The Angelus, 1979

Pauline with the first Angelus resident. At the Special Olympics, 1982

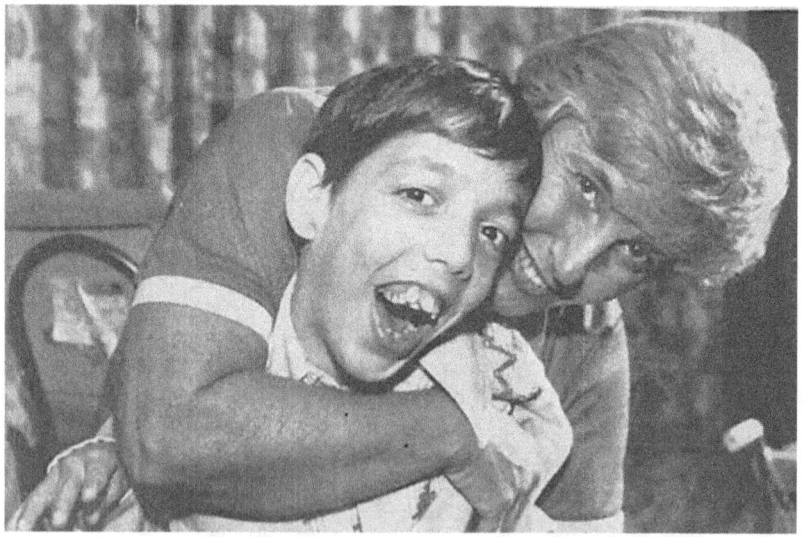

Resident in Pauline's warm embrace. *St. Petersburg Times* article, 1983
(Photo: Ricardo Ferro)

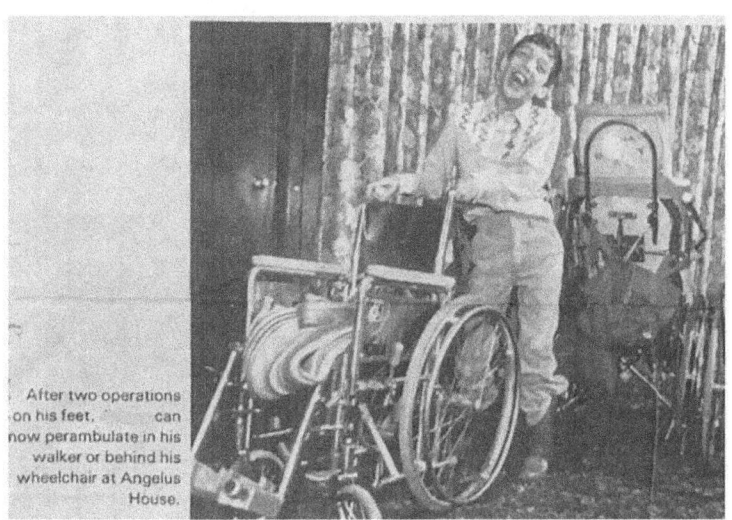

After two operations on his feet, can now perambulate in his walker or behind his wheelchair at Angelus House.

Newspaper article about a resident at The Angelus *St. Petersburg Times* article by Roy Peter Clark ,1983 (Photo: Ricardo Ferro)

Last year, Pete had to wheel himself to the finish line. This year he can walk.

Resident participating in the Special Olympics *St. Petersburg Times* article by Roy Peter Clark ,1983 (Photo: Ricardo Ferro)

His spirit freed him from an institution; his mission now is to save his brother

Newspaper article about a resident. *St. Petersburg Times* article
by Roy Peter Clark, 1985 (Photo: Ricardo Ferro)

Dave Shaver, Pauline's husband, 1986

Pauline and Dave's Wedding Day with sons, Marty and Joe, 1986

Pauline and Dave's Wedding Day with daughter, Perri, 1986

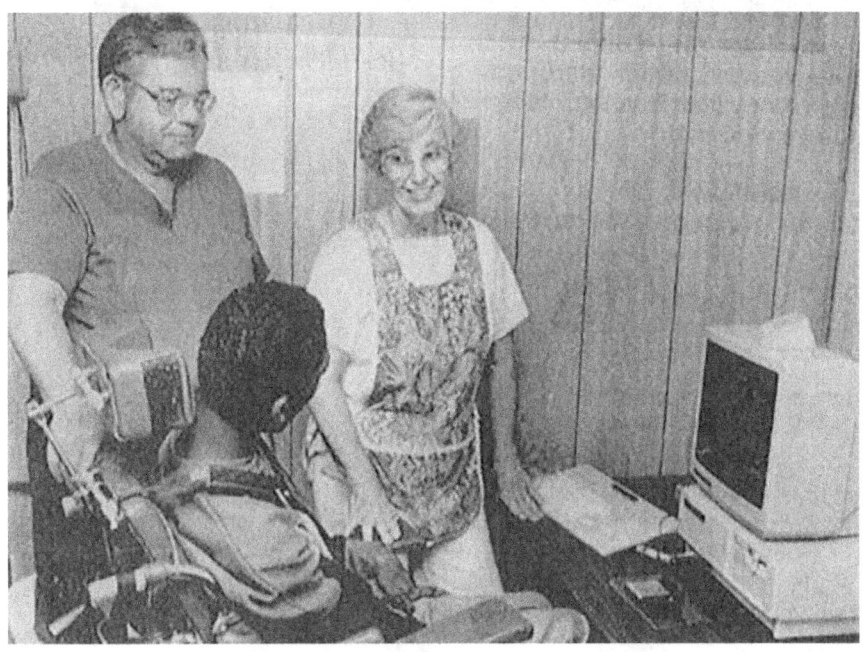

Pauline and Dave, Computer Class at the ADT Center
The Tampa Tribune, 1988 (Photo: Jay Conner)

Equine Therapy: Horseback Riding Program, 1988

Volunteers building Charlie's Lodge, 1999

Resident with Pauline Construction site of Charlie's Lodge, 1999

Pauline and Dave adding the last log. Charlie's Lodge construction, 1999

The beautiful, brand-new Charlie's Lodge, 1999

Charlie's Lodge interior, 1999

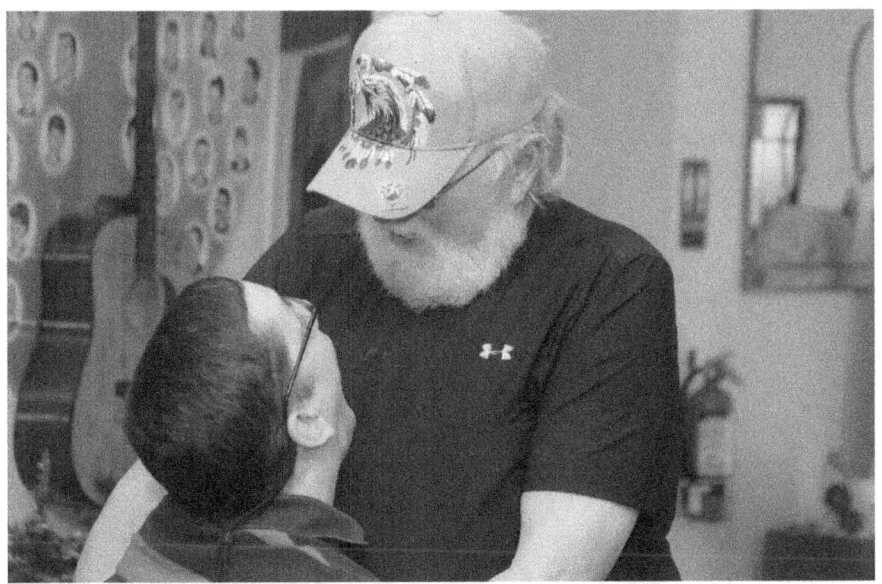

One of Charlie Daniels' many visits with a resident, 2004

Charlie Daniels at a Christmas Party with the residents, 2004

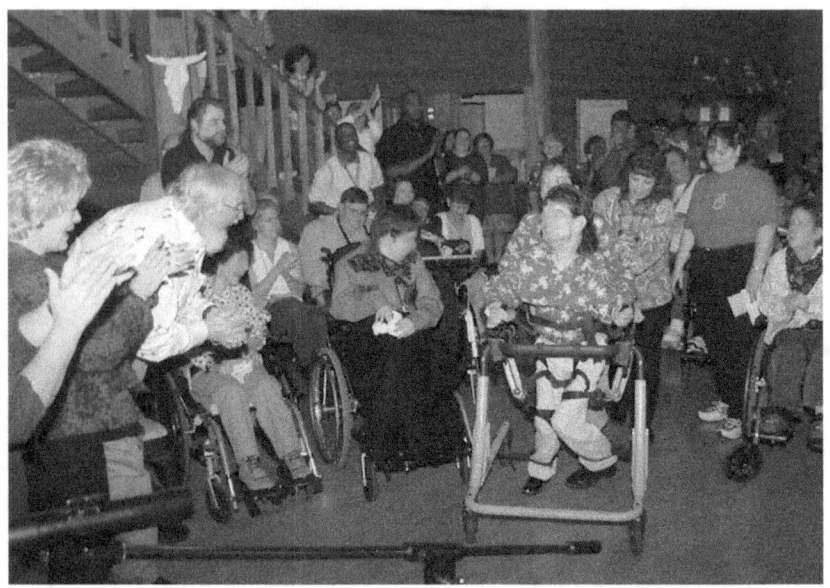

Residents welcoming Hazel and Charlie Daniels Charlie's Lodge, 2004

Charlie's Lodge Dining Room with residents, 2005

The Angelus Christmas Pageant with the Angel Choir, 2005

Light Up The Angelus Annual Holiday Event, 2024

Pauline, Charlie and Dave, 2006

Charlie Daniels' Benefit Concert for The Angelus, 2006

ADT Gardening Class, 2013

Resident on a Wheelchair Accessible Swing, 2013

Residents heading to The Angelus Annual Picnic, 2013

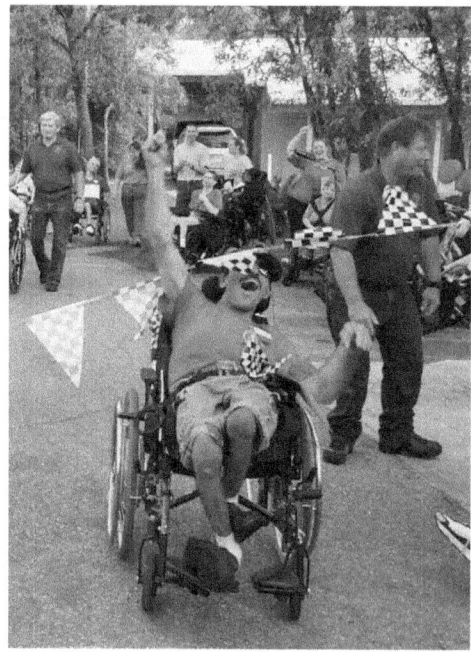

The Angelus Wheelchair Race, 2014 Winner at the finish line!

Pauline rides with a Motorcycle Club volunteer, 2017

The sprawling grounds of The Angelus Campus, 2025

Entrance sign to The Angelus Campus, Hudson, FL, 2025

PART TWO

WE HAVE A FARM!

THE ANGELUS EXPANDS ITS WINGS

By 1984, The Angelus had outgrown its original home in St. Petersburg, surpassing its licensed limit of twelve children. Faced with the need to expand, I began searching for a more rural setting that could accommodate the growing family. I had been thinking about a farm for a long time and even shared my dream with Pete during some of our morning conversations. After several fruitless trips, I found a promising seventeen-acre property in Hudson, Pasco County. It was located a few miles from civilization on a lime rock-dusted tree-lined road. The ride was so bumpy it rattled my teeth. The price was right, and the owner's name was Mr. Sweet, and with a name like that I just knew he would accept my offer. With faith and urgency, I signed the papers and declared: We have a farm!

As fate would have it, several neighbors had personal connections to the St. Petersburg community, affirming the sense that this was the right place. Across the street was the Harker family from the parish of Holy Name, and whose kids attended the school where I had been the PE teacher and coach! Another neighbor was Betty Williams, a retired PE teacher from St. John's School at St. Pete Beach. I knew Betty very well as we competed in sports activities. When I told her what I was doing, she invited me to come up and bring a few of the kids so they could see "the farm." A picnic visit with some of the children confirmed that Hudson would be our new home.

Betty and Walt Williams's little house was right on a lake that had a lot of fish; they had plenty of rabbits and a black Labrador named BT because he had a bent tail. Next to them was a family with chickens, a horse, and a cow named "Hamburger." I learned that the other neighboring property to the Williams's was a five-acre parcel with a barn and two small houses, owned by a man named Dave Shaver.

All these connections with my past felt like a sign that I was making the right decision. The transition wasn't without challenges, but it was full of momentum. To purchase the property, I had to find a lawyer to complete the transaction. Steve Booth would prove to be more than a good lawyer; he became a friend, supporter, and beloved Chair of our board. Now that we had the land, we needed to build a house. I found a contractor who worked with me to modify the layout to accommodate the special requirements we needed for our angels. And because we needed special permits, Steve was right there for us.

As work progressed, I couldn't help but notice how close our property was to the lake and how much our children would enjoy having access to it. I decided to knock on the door of our neighbor, Dave, to see if we might be able to visit from time to time. "Sure thing," he said warmly, "but I should tell you, I'm selling the place to move closer to my job."

It turned out Dave's land included five beautiful acres with a barn, two homes (one new and one old), and that coveted stretch of lakefront. It was as if the missing piece of the vision had revealed itself. I could see it clearly now: sidewalks connecting the homes, a barn, gardens, and yes, the lake just as I had imagined, just like the picture Perri had painted for me. I brought the idea to our board, and they said "yes" to purchasing the additional five acres.

At the time, it felt like a practical and hopeful expansion of our dream. Little did I know that knocking on Dave Shaver's door would open far more than access to the lake.

I moved with three children into a house on the newly acquired property, while the first Angelus house was being built. The Angelus in

St. Pete was well taken care of with Perri, my sister Lou, and new house parents Linda and Travis. In Hudson, support came from many directions, friends, neighbors, even the SeaBees Reserve, under the direction of Captain George Constantine, who cleared land during their summer duty. The new location quickly earned the nickname "Angelus Country," and the first home was built. Dave and Jerry built a little red barn to house and hide the water tank we had to get for the fire sprinkler system. I remember that we tried to get a grant to pay for this very expensive water tank, but we were denied because we weren't licensed when we applied. Just another one of those challenges I was able to deal with because of the newfound Hudson community of friends and neighbors. And every time I look at that sweet red barn, I am reminded of the kindness and support The Angelus received. With the transition complete, The Angelus began a new chapter in Hudson, continuing its mission of care and dignity for those who needed it most.

JERRY THOMAS:
THE CARPENTER OF NEW BEGINNINGS

J erry Thomas was a carpenter and painter who became an integral part of The Angelus. His journey with us began when Dan Wilson, our accountant, benefactor, and a close family friend hired him to paint our house on Castile Way South in St. Petersburg. This was no ordinary painting job. With all twelve of our children living at home, Jerry had to navigate the chaos and joy that comes with such a bustling household. His workday revolved around the children's school schedule; the bus arrived at 7:15 a.m. to whisk them away and returned them home by 3:00 p.m. Every day, Jerry would witness the transformative energy of our kids returning home, thrilled to leave their wheelchairs behind and dive into the simple pleasures of childhood. Over time, he grew fond of the lively atmosphere and the camaraderie of the family.

On the acquisition of the property in Hudson, we struck a deal with Jerry to become the groundskeeper in exchange for a home for his wife and elderly mother-in-law. By then, he had retired from his career and was ready for a quieter pace. He took to the task with his usual dedication, transforming an abandoned house on the property into a cozy home, a place we now call "Jerry House." Jerry poured his heart into the land, mowing the sprawling grounds and restoring life to an old barn cluttered with rusty tools and forgotten farm equipment left by the previous owner.

Meanwhile, I had moved into the main house on the property, bringing three of our children from St. Petersburg: Sam, Marcus, and

Chase. With Jerry and his family nearby, I felt safe in this wilderness as I began overseeing the development of our seventeen acres and the construction of our first house. Back in St. Petersburg, our home was well-managed by Perri, Lou, and the new house parents, ensuring the rest of our children were cared for. I also worked with the Pasco County school system to prepare them for the arrival of twelve new students with disabilities.

Jerry's connection with our family deepened during this time. He often watched over Sam, Marcus, and Chase while I attended church or ran errands. His gentle presence was a source of comfort for all of us. It wasn't long before our little family grew. Two weeks into our new life in Hudson, Child Protective Services brought us Miles, a handsome young man who was non-ambulatory and non-verbal. Miles quickly became a part of our family, joining Sam, Marcus, and Chase as one of the first residents of Florence House. This home, built on our "farm," marked the beginning of a new chapter for The Angelus.

Jerry's story is woven into the very fabric of this chapter. He wasn't just a groundskeeper; he was a pillar of support and a reminder of the extraordinary people who helped us build a place of love and opportunity for those who needed it most. As Florence House became a home, and our family expanded, Jerry remained a steadfast presence, a quiet hero in the story of The Angelus.

MILES:
A JOURNEY OF GROWTH,
DETERMINATION, AND INDEPENDENCE

Miles, a bright, handsome twelve-year-old boy, came to us just before Florence House was completed, spending his first days in the original Dave House alongside Sam, Marcus, and Chase until his new home was ready. He had been living with his mother and older brother in a nearby town. Though his world was shaped by significant challenges, his presence was full of warmth and quiet determination. He was non-verbal, and his severely tightened muscles made it hard for him to control his arms and legs.

For his safety, he sometimes needed to be restrained in his wheelchair to prevent accidental movements that could knock over objects or unintentionally strike those around him. But despite this burden, his spirit was cooperative and kind, always trying his best to regulate his movements. Even when things went wrong, like knocking over a drink or jostling a nearby table, the remorse in his eyes was unmistakable. He cared deeply about the people around him.

Daily routines required patience and adaptation. Miles had a strong appetite but needed full assistance at every meal. He eagerly drank from a cup when held for him, though some spillage was inevitable. Dressing and personal care involved careful teamwork, especially given his heightened muscle tightness. With time, routine, and trust, Miles became more at ease and comfortable. Thinking about Miles, what stands out most is how he met every challenge with determination, never letting his limitations define him.

Miles attended a local elementary school for students with special needs, where he quickly became a favorite among his teachers and classmates. Later, he graduated from high school, a major milestone that reflected both his perseverance and the unwavering support of those who believed in him.

Miles thrived at The Angelus. He grew tall and strong, engaging in every opportunity that came his way. I remember how his determination shone through when he competed in the Special Olympics. He found joy in concerts and activities, sharing in the laughter and camaraderie of his housemates. His friendships were real, and his laugh unforgettable. Miles left a lasting impact on everyone he met.

After nearly a decade, Miles's mother made the thoughtful decision to support his next chapter. With excitement and optimism, Miles moved back to his nearby hometown to live with his older brother in an apartment. Miles embraced his new independence with the same enthusiasm and determination that had always defined him.

A few years later, he stopped by for a visit. I saw how confident this young man had become. His mother beamed with pride, full of stories and smiles. She spoke about his life, a life he was actively shaping with courage and independence. Watching him that day, I understood that the foundation built at The Angelus had been one part of a much larger story, one written by Miles himself. With the love of his family, the belief of his teachers, and the friendships he was building a life full of independence, growth, and love.

DAVE SHAVER:
PARTNER, INNOVATOR, AND BUILDER

D ave Shaver is a remarkable man who became not only my partner and husband but also an essential figure in the growth and
success of The Angelus in Hudson. His dedication, innovation, and
quiet strength helped build the foundation that allowed The Angelus
to thrive.

By the time I settled on the seventeen-acre property in Pasco
County for the next chapter of The Angelus, I already felt a sense of
destiny unfolding: neighbors with ties to my past, a peaceful rural setting, and a vision for what this place could become. But there was one
missing piece: the lake. Little John Lake shimmered just beyond our
reach, part of the adjoining property next door.

One afternoon, hoping for nothing more than a bit of kindness, I
walked over and knocked on the neighbor's door. That neighbor was
Dave Shaver. I asked if he might allow our children to access the lake
now and then. With an easy smile, he said, "Sure thing," but casually
added that he was planning to sell the property and move closer to his
job. That simple exchange opened the door to a much larger opportunity, not just for The Angelus, but for my own life.

The property Dave was selling included five more acres, a barn,
two modest houses, and, of course, that stretch of lakefront. With the
board's support, the purchase was approved. The Angelus was growing

again; this time with a barn, a lake, and a door that had only just opened.

At the time, I thought I was just securing the final piece of the dream. What I didn't yet know was that the man who made it possible would become such a central part of it. At first, it was all business; discussing survey lines, property boundaries, and construction plans. Then we began having coffee now and then and chatting over the phone. They were casual chats at first, about work, the weather, and the lake. But the conversations stretched longer. We talked about family, the lives we had led, and the turns we didn't expect. There was no grand declaration, no movie moment, just a steady unfolding. A kind of trust that built itself day by day.

Dave's mind was always working. He served in the Navy, where he trained in radar systems, and later continued at Honeywell, gaining a deep understanding of programming and computer technology. He eventually joined Consteel in Clearwater, creating designs and cost analyses for steel construction jobs. Even on paper, he was impressive, but it was his heart and humility that made him unforgettable.

Dave and his mother had sung in the church choir before he joined the Navy. After she passed away just before his discharge, his church family, the McLauchlins, unofficially adopted him. Every summer and holiday, they camped together in Hudson, Florida, where Dave eventually bought five acres of land. On weekends, he was joined by his adopted family, raising chickens and rabbits and "playing farm." It was through the McLauchlins that Dave met George Constantine, the owner of a steel fabrication company. That connection helped launch Dave's career in engineering and sparked his passion for designing computer programs. And as much as he loved his farm life, commuting to work became costly. This is what prompted Dave to sell his property.

Dave was never just "the guy next door." He had a quiet steadiness about him, a practical kindness that made you feel like everything might actually work out. He'd stop by the construction site just to check on the progress, lend a tool, or ask if we needed anything from town. Dave's compassion and ingenuity became evident when he started volunteering, offering to set up a communication system for Sam, one of our residents. He visited us in St. Petersburg to create a large, interactive "book" with colorful buttons that Sam could press with his fist to answer yes-and-no questions. Over time, Sam progressed from basic communication to using a computer with specialized programs Dave designed to teach him science, geography, and math.

Dave also helped me establish a computer-based mailing list for my newsletters. This was all new to me, and Dave patiently taught me the basics of computer language and programming. He quickly bonded with our residents, displaying a deep understanding and interest in their lives. It wasn't long before he became a familiar, comforting presence, someone who could fix a broken light switch, reprogram a computer, and hold a resident's hand, all in the same afternoon.

Recognizing Dave's kindness, intelligence, and quiet strength, I invited my three children to dinner to meet him. Although he was a lifelong bachelor and a bit shy, our friendship blossomed into love. I initially worried that fostering twelve children with disabilities might be overwhelming for him, but he embraced it wholeheartedly. My children approved, and on March 1, 1986, we married at Dave's church in St. Petersburg. The ceremony was beautiful: Perri was my maid of honor, my sister Lou was the bridesmaid, and my two sons, Joe and Marty, walked me down the aisle. Dave's best friend, Carl McLauchlin, was his best man, and his longtime boss, George Constantine, served as his attendant. Some joked that Dave married me just to get his property back, but we all knew it was much more than that.

As our first house, Florence House, was being built in Hudson, Dave took on the role of project manager while continuing to work at Consteel. Florence House became home to four boys: Sam, Marcus, Chase, and Miles. Meanwhile, Perri and Lou managed operations in

St. Petersburg. When house parents Linda and Travis moved on, we decided to bring all our children together in Hudson.

Dave worked closely with Steve Booth and a newly formed committee to build our second house. Although he still commuted to Clearwater, he devoted evenings and weekends to construction, leading volunteers who had little experience but a lot of enthusiasm. Despite the challenges, the house was completed in record time.

When our day program was established, Dave resigned from Consteel and took on the role of computer instructor. He designed custom programs tailored to each resident's learning abilities, helping them develop new skills. He also partnered with Jerry in maintaining our growing facilities, ensuring everything from plumbing to electrical work was handled efficiently.

Dave became my main assistant, cheerfully taking on any job I asked of him. He joined me on grocery runs, managed logistics, and kept everything in order. Despite his essential role, he always stayed in the background, shying away from interviews and public recognition. He never sought the spotlight but remained a steadfast force behind the success of The Angelus.

Dave's contributions to The Angelus are immeasurable. They are etched into every wall, woven into every program, and felt in every room. He taught by example how to listen, how to solve, and how to serve. His work made life better for our residents, but his presence made life sweeter for all of us. He was my partner, my teammate, and my home. And though he never wanted a spotlight, his love lit the path forward for me, for the Angelus, and for everyone lucky enough to walk beside him. I miss him every day.

STEVE BOOTH:
A PILLAR OF THE ANGELUS COMMUNITY

I first met Steve Booth when I approached him for help purchasing land in Hudson. I brought Sam with me to that first meeting. He was the oldest in our care at the time and the only one not attending school, so he often came along on errands. That day, as we sat in Steve's office, Sam was nestled comfortably in his stroller, grinning and playfully flirting with Steve's beautiful secretary, sending messages with those expressive eyes of his, as only he could.

Steve was instantly taken with Sam and asked me what I was planning to do with the land. I told him I wanted to create a place where children with complex needs could live and grow, a true home. "This community needs a cause to rally behind," he said. And he meant it. From that day on, Steve Booth became one of our fiercest advocates.

He handled all the legal work for the land, including the trickiest part, securing a zoning variance from Pasco County. At the time, the property was zoned only for agricultural and residential use. Creating a group home for children with disabilities—especially through a nonprofit—required a formal petition and a public hearing before the zoning board. Some neighbors objected. They didn't understand what we were trying to build. There was fear, not malice, but it still hurt. People assumed the worst, that these children would somehow disrupt their quiet lives.

Steve stepped up to represent us.

I brought Mara with me to the zoning board meeting in her wheeel-chair. She was always radiant, with a smile that could melt even the ici-est of rooms. Steve, confident and composed in front of the Board of County Commissioners, spoke about the need for compassion in our county, and about children like Mara who deserved a safe and loving place to call home. When he mentioned that some folks thought she might be a threat, Mara burst into the sweetest giggles. Her joy was contagious. Even the most stone-faced board members cracked a smile.

The hearing ended in victory. With Steve's legal know-how and our shared vision, the board voted in our favor. We were granted the vari-ance. We had the green light to build The Angelus.

Things started moving quickly after that. Our first home, built by a professional contractor, was finished just before Christmas. On one visit, Steve showed up with a live Christmas tree and a toy train set to circle it, a symbol of joy and new beginnings. The house was named Florence House in honor of my mother, who had passed away the year before. Steve met the children living there and after that visit, he was all in.

When I told Steve about the ten children still living in St. Petersburg and how hard it was to manage things from a distance, he jumped into action. He formed a committee of local professionals who generously donated their time and expertise. An architect replicated the design of the first house, a neighbor cleared the land and supplied truckloads of dirt, and numerous contractors, masons, plumbers, electricians, and community members lent a hand. Dave and Jerry worked tirelessly, shoulder to shoulder with the volunteers, keeping the job site orderly and moving smoothly. Every bit of material and labor was donated. From April 4 to August 20, 1987, that house rose from the dirt, built entirely by goodwill.

By September, the painting was done, furniture had been delivered, and our kids were able to move in just in time for school. We named it Booth House in heartfelt gratitude for Steve's extraordinary efforts.

But Steve didn't stop there. He went on to Chair our Board of Directors for the next forty years. Under his leadership, The Angelus expanded and thrived. We added a heated swimming pool, another home, an adult day program center, a log cabin lodge, and a beautiful open-air pavilion for outdoor activities. Whenever we ran into zoning issues or needed permits, Steve was right there, helping us navigate the red tape all the while making sure we preserved the "war chest" that Jerry Seaborn had worked so hard to build.

So many of these projects were made possible by community groups: civic clubs like the Rotary Club of New Port Richey, the Optimists, the Kiwanis, Beacon Community Church, the Interact Club from the Diocese of St. Petersburg, the Women Marines, Boy Scouts, and Fred Deuel Surveying Company, which donated a full survey of all seventeen acres. Steve knew so many people in our community and could recruit volunteers for every aspect of our growth.

Even during disagreements, Steve had a talent for diplomacy. He listened. He brought people back to the table and reminded them why we were doing this in the first place. When board members stepped down, he quietly found the right people to take their place, always with the mission in mind.

And when celebrities like Charlie Daniels and others came on board, Steve made sure everything was by the book. He handled permits, event logistics, contracts; you name it. December was his marathon month, overseeing multiple events for visiting celebrities. Gar and Tammy Williams co-chaired those programs with him, making sure everything ran smoothly. Steve even managed the live auctions at our annual banquet, personally ensuring every donated item and dollar was accounted for. Throughout the year, he was constantly on the lookout for benefactors to contribute to The Angelus.

He wasn't just our lawyer. Steve Booth was our compass, our bridge to the broader community, and our steady hand in moments of uncertainty. His legacy runs through every building, every tree, and every life touched by The Angelus.

BRICK BY BRICK:
EXPANDING HOPE
THROUGH COMMUNITY

Booth House was finally completed, and all the children were together at last. Florence House had started with just four residents, then two more joined, and the remaining ten moved into Booth House. We already had a waiting list, and now that we were fully settled in Hudson, new faces began to arrive. Mary came first, followed by Gloria and Charles, dear friends from our earlier days in St. Petersburg.

Our younger residents attended school in New Port Richey, where the local program for students with special needs extended through age twenty-two. But we also saw a growing need for a daytime program for our young adults who had finished school. So, we repurposed a donated double-wide trailer into our very first Adult Day Training (ADT) center. Dave and Jerry transformed that humble trailer into a vibrant space for learning and laughter. It was the start of yet another meaningful chapter in The Angelus story. A beautiful article even ran in the local paper, celebrating the launch of our program.

Thanks to Dave and Jerry, the space was thoughtfully designed: a kitchen for home economics classes, a dedicated room for Dave's computer lessons, divided into zones, one for music and physical activities, the other for arts and crafts. There was a handicapped–accessible bathroom, a front office with its own entrance for my sister, Lucille (whom everyone called "Aunt Lou"), and a long outside ramp leading to six raised garden beds for our gardening program. Staff, not teachers, were eventually hired, and I wrote "lesson plans" for each class.

Dave developed creative, adaptive tools so that every student could participate: chin switches for some, foot switches for others, and the big red switch for the rest.

Our first "students" were the residents we already knew and loved: Sam, Mara (a recent graduate from St. Petersburg), Gloria, and Mary, each one ready for a new routine filled with activity and purpose. But our doors soon opened wider. Word spread fast, and soon we were welcoming community members from across the county, individuals with similar needs who still lived at home with their families but had few options during the day. Walter, Norman, Grant, Rose, and Cheryl; each one bright, curious, and expressive in their own way joined us daily via the county bus. All used wheelchairs, and all brought something beautiful and unique to the program. They were deeply engaged and eager to connect and participate. Each morning, just after the sun had cleared the tops of the trees, the quiet hum of the county bus signaled a new day at our adult day training center. The staff would pause whatever they were doing and move to the front door, where the real heart of the day was about to begin.

The side doors of the bus folded open with a soft hiss, and the mechanical whirr of the chairlift filled the air, ready for its precious cargo. One by one, our community students made their descent. The lift rose and lowered, rose and lowered, transforming a moment that could have felt clinical or routine into something meaningful and full of grace. Each arrival was its own ceremony of welcome; an act of trust and care that set the tone for everything that came after.

Their arrival brought new energy to the program and a deep sense of purpose to our work. For their parents, this was more than a day program, it was a lifeline. The few hours of respite we could offer gave them a chance to rest, work, or simply breathe, knowing their loved ones were in caring, capable hands.

We embraced the challenge of meeting each person's needs, learning together what worked, what sparked joy, and what helped everyone feel seen, heard, and included. It wasn't always easy, but it was deeply rewarding; brick by brick, we were building something far bigger than a day program. We were building community.

Each morning at the ADT center began with a shared moment of unity. Everyone gathered, including Aunt Lou, to say the Pledge of Allegiance; the students with hands over hearts if they were able, others with assistance from staff who stood beside them, gently guiding the motion. What followed was music, always music. The music teacher made sure every student had an instrument in hand, or helped them find a way to participate, offering support to those who needed help interacting with their instruments. The rhythm was loud and gloriously unsynchronized: maracas shaking at odd intervals, tambourines clashing off-beat, and drums thumping with wild abandon. It wasn't exactly in key or in time, but it didn't matter. The sound was full of life, laughter, the unmistakable sound of a joyful noise! These mornings didn't just start the day, they lifted it.

Lunchtime was another moment of togetherness. Everyone gathered at the tables to eat, side by side. Before meals, Bob led the group in a familiar grace, his voice steady and warm: "God our Father" (God our Father), "once again" (once again), "we will ask your blessing" (we will ask your blessing), "Amen!" (Amen!). The simple, sweet ritual echoed with laughter and a chorus of voices repeating after him. It was a moment of reverence and routine that grounded the group in gratitude.

In the afternoons, the community came alive again through the animal and gardening programs, two of the most beloved parts of the day. The ADT center had been gifted three miniature horses by the Miniature Horse Association; three gentle, curious animals who stood just the right height for a wheelchair-bound student to meet them eye to eye. Alongside the horses were goats, birds, and a bunny, all lovingly tended by a teacher who understood that ability looked different for everyone. She found ways for each student to contribute, brushing the horses with brushes strapped to their feet, pulling small wagons of hay with ropes carefully tied for easier grip. Every movement, every effort, was met with encouragement. It wasn't about perfection; it was about connection.

In the garden, another teacher patiently worked with students to get their hands into the dirt, planting seeds and tending raised beds designed specifically to accommodate wheelchairs. Vines grew along trellises—cucumbers, beans, tomatoes—within reach of curious hands. And when hands couldn't reach on their own, someone was always there to guide and assist. Every student got to experience the sensation of soil, the satisfaction of watering, and the joy of harvesting what they helped grow.

I remember standing there, watching it all unfold, and thinking how lucky I was to have these wonderful teachers by my side. What started as ideas scribbled on paper was now coming to life right before my eyes. But it was more than just a dream realized; it was a revelation. These weren't just daily activities to fill time. They were sacred moments of dignity, joy, and connection between students and staff; between effort and reward; between the human heart and the community that embraced it. In that little center, tucked away in Hudson, every person found a way to belong. And so did I.

Walter and Norman, brothers in their forties, were a unique pair. Their mother made sure Walter had four cigarettes a day. He'd tuck them in his shirt pocket and ration them out to Norman like clockwork. They wheeled themselves between classes, curious and independent, exploring the program's offerings. Rose was highly verbal and full of spirit, often flirting with the boys, though they learned quickly to keep moving. Grant, an avid reader, took on the role of reading a chapter of *Moby Dick* daily out loud to those interested. He also developed a fondness for our Home Economics teacher, never letting a day pass without a formal goodbye at the bus door. Every one of them brought something special and their differences blended into a rich, beautiful community.

As our program gained recognition, more families reached out. With the help of state social workers and Aunt Lou's meticulous bookkeeping, we secured funding for the day program. But the billing calculated by the quarter-hour became a real challenge. And government funding, as always, came with complications. When Florence House was under construction, we discovered we needed a fire sprinkler system. Living in a rural area with no water system, we purchased a pressurized water tank. Though a grant for this system was initially approved, it was later denied because we were not yet a licensed facility. A disheartening setback.

Similarly, once we began accepting community students, the county eliminated transportation funding altogether. The need didn't go away, and I wasn't about to close our doors to those students and those families, so I did what I had to do and became the driver, personally transporting Walter, Norman, Grant, Cheryl, and Rose to and from the center each day.

I was determined to not only keep our program open but expand it. Leaning on community support, we began hosting fundraisers, while our board of directors organized the construction of a brand-new 50 x 100-foot building for the ADT. On build–day, more than twenty-five masons arrived, and brick by brick, the walls went up. By noon, every single block, all donated, I might add, had been laid. Our wheelchair-using residents gathered nearby, joyfully cheering on the volunteers.

That building was a blessing. It had four accessible bathrooms, a commercial kitchen, a laundry room with a built-in tub, a reception area, a business office, a stage used for physical therapy, and a large cafeteria that seated forty students. It allowed us to expand and welcome more adults, including those from Zephyrhills who had no access to similar programs. Some came just to bathe, as their aging parents could no longer lift them. Unfortunately, their transportation funding was also cut, and I couldn't make these longer trips. So, while our day program continued for our residents, many others lost access to vital care.

Still, we pressed on. A third house was built with the help of our friend Ann Ahern, providing a beautiful home for students like Walter, Norman, Grant, Don, Jack, and Travis, all of whom attended the day program. By this time, The Angelus had grown to house twenty-six permanent residents.

Through it all—the victories, the setbacks, the hard-won progress—we kept building. Not just buildings, but a way of life. A home. A family. A Place where every person was seen, loved, and lifted.

JERRY SEABORN:
A STEWARD OF INTEGRITY AND HEART

Jerry Seaborn was one of our first members of the board of directors in St. Petersburg. He was very quiet but immensely knowledge-able about finances and investments, working as a stockbroker for a well-known company. Father Goodman, who was also on our board and my boss at Holy Name School, where I taught physical education, often consulted Jerry on his personal finances. Father Goodman received such good advice from Jerry that it sealed my confidence and trust in him.

After we moved to Hudson, at our first annual picnic, Jerry arrived with two elderly sisters who were his clients. I was introduced to the sisters and discovered they had been schoolteachers, leading to a delightful conversation about teaching. I gave them a tour of our facilities, and they had the opportunity to meet our children. The following week, Jerry called to inform me that the sisters had donated $250,000 to us through him. The board was ecstatic, and Jerry carefully invested that donation, ensuring its growth.

Thanks to the stewardship of Jerry Seaborn and Steve Booth, our board of directors has cultivated this nest egg to safeguard the Angelus' mission: to provide those entrusted to our care with a place to live, to love, and to learn. Over the years, board members in both St. Petersburg and Hudson have continued to protect the funds raised through Charlie Daniels events and other initiatives. These efforts have included raffles for motorcycles, cars, and other prizes, as well as wine-tasting parties and "Shootouts" in Pasco County, which raised thousands of dollars alongside the Charlie Daniels events. Under the leadership of Joe Neri, we also developed a Christmas extravaganza called "Light Up The Angelus," featuring millions of lights and blow-ups to illuminate the entire property. This event has grown every year and is now our primary fundraiser.

When COVID-19 hit, our fundraising efforts diminished significantly, and staffing became a crisis. Many staff members had to stay home to care for their families, leaving our remaining loyal staff stretched to their limits. Despite their incredible dedication, we could not provide the raises they deserved due to dwindling funds. Meanwhile, navigating state and federal funding became a nightmare as we had to prove that The Angelus was not an institution; an inquisition that lasted over a year and cost us both time and money.

Recruiting new staff proved nearly impossible, as many found it easier to stay home and collect federal benefits. To cope, we had to condense our homes to a manageable number, ensuring we could provide basic care with our existing staff. The Lodge and Dave House no longer housed residents but retained their licensing criteria in hopes of resuming operations in the future.

In this crisis, our board of directors assumed additional responsibilities to continue fundraising while minimizing the use of our nest egg. The government's budget cuts have made it increasingly difficult to operate as we aspired to, but we remained steadfast in our mission. With faith and determination, we continued to persevere, knowing that brighter days lie ahead.

WITH LOVE, FROM GINNY

Ginny came to us on the recommendation of Irene in 1986, one of our first employees at Florence House. A petite Chinese woman with a quiet presence and a quick smile, Ginny's English was limited when she started, though she had already lived in Hudson for ten years. Her husband, Ming, worked as a cook at the local Chinese restaurant, and their two children were students at the neighborhood elementary school.

From the beginning, Ginny brought warmth, humility, and a relentless work ethic. She began at Florence House and was soon watching Booth House take shape next door. Despite the language barrier, she jumped into her duties with enthusiasm, learning G-tube feedings and other medical care with remarkable speed. I once told her the kids might have a hard time understanding her, and she laughed, "It's okay, Miss Pauline; I don't understand them either!"

Back then, a high school diploma wasn't required for direct care work, but Ginny insisted on furthering her education. With help from her children, she enrolled in evening classes at the local high school and studied diligently to improve her English. She earned her GED by her second year and learned to write daily case notes, document medications properly, and communicate more confidently with families and staff.

Ginny became an essential part of our team, always on time, dependable, and generous in every way. When Booth House opened, she transferred there and helped train new staff, learning all about the ten children who had moved from St. Petersburg. She pulled double shifts without complaint, mastered the unique ways each resident communicated, and brought Ming's famous egg rolls to every party (though she proudly insisted hers were even better). We were regularly surprised with lovingly prepared Chinese food, always served with a smile.

She often shared stories of her childhood in a small mountain village in China. Her father had two wives, one with ten children, the other with eight, and they all lived under one roof. Ginny had loved school but was pulled out after fifth grade to help in the home. Her voice always held a mix of pride and wistfulness when she spoke of those early years of gardens, family chores, and a deep longing to learn.

Ginny filled every role we asked of her and then some. But one trip stands out as a true window into the depth of her commitment and her joy.

Dave and I had planned a road trip with Pete and Sam, an adventure to show them the mountains and landmarks they had always dreamed of seeing. Dave modified our van, installing two lounge chairs by the windows and a bed in the back for comfort and G-tube care. We invited Ginny to come along, and she eagerly said yes.

She wasn't just there to help. She was part of the family.

From the moment we set out, Ginny was in her element, helping care for the boys, yes, but also singing along to patriotic songs, snapping photos, asking questions, and marveling at the sights. In Washington, D.C., we met our local representatives, toured the White House, rode the subway, and stood in awe before the statue of Abraham Lincoln. At a military band concert in a sprawling park, Ginny kept pace with Dave, singing every song at the top of her lungs while Pete and Sam tapped their feet in rhythm. Sam even tried to sing along. On the way home we detoured to explore some caves, laughing and marveling like kids on a school trip.

Ginny never lost that wonder. She brought it with her into every room, every shift, every conversation. She's just as proud of her adopted country as she is of the family she and Ming raised. Her son graduated valedictorian, earned a full scholarship, and now travels the world as a bridge consultant with a doctorate in engineering. Her daughter graduated with honors, started a family, and blessed Ginny with two beautiful grandchildren. She beams with pride at every school recital and shares photos like any proud grandma, still humble, still joyful, still deeply rooted in love.

Now, thirty-nine years later, Ginny still works weekends. We all wish we could clone her. She's the heart of Ann House; the one who makes the best egg rolls, sings with gusto, and welcomes everyone she meets like an old friend. Her beloved Ming is gone now, and so is my dear Dave. But if they were still here, I have no doubt we'd be planning another incredible road trip with Ginny right there beside us singing, smiling, and holding everything together with quiet, steady grace.

BROOKE:
A LIFE OF STRENGTH
AND UNWAVERING SPIRIT

Brooke first came to The Angelus for short-term respite care. She and her mother had recently relocated from out of state, and her mom was navigating the maze of Health and Rehabilitative Services (HRS) and the still-new Medicaid waiver system. It was a mess of red tape and forms, loopholes, and waiting lists. Honestly, it was hard enough for seasoned case workers to make sense of it, let alone a parent trying to advocate for her child. My heart went out to her.

From the moment Brooke arrived, we knew she was someone special. Sharp and observant, she didn't need words to make herself understood. Though she was non-verbal, her eyes said everything. She zipped around confidently in her power chair, and while she had a word board beside her, she preferred gestures and facial expressions, along with a series of well-timed yes-or-no questions to get her point across.

And if you misunderstood her, she never got frustrated. She'd just give a quick little shake of her head—her gentle "nope, try again"—and then flash you the brightest smile, tapping her hand lightly on her wheelchair tray like she was saying, "Oh well, you're close; let's give it another shot." That grace, that patience, that generosity of spirit, made you want to keep trying until you got it right. And when you did, when the light bulb went off and you finally figured out what she was trying to say, her entire face would shine with joy, as if the two of you had just accomplished something truly wonderful together.

Though Brooke came from a privileged background—her stepfather had given her every tool for independence, including a cell phone, stylish clothes, and even hair dye in fun colors that matched her vibrant personality—she never carried herself with entitlement. It was more of a quiet confidence, a sense of self-grounded not in what she had, but in who she was.

She settled into life at The Angelus with warmth and grace, quickly forming bonds with her housemates and staff. Beloved for her spirit and her sense of humor, Brooke could make anyone feel welcome.

When her mother passed away suddenly it was a devastating blow, but Brooke's family remained close. Her stepfather continued to be a steady and loving presence. He had already purchased a fully accessible van with a lift so Brooke could enjoy family outings, and after her mother's passing, he remained deeply involved by checking in, showing up, and supporting The Angelus quietly and generously, never seeking recognition.

Brooke embraced life in her new home and community with curiosity and courage. She loved attending concerts, wrestling events, and any kind of social gathering. That smile of hers and her open heart drew people in. Musicians and visitors remembered her by name, and more than one band member lingered after a show just to sit and chat with her a little longer. She had that kind of presence; magnetic, but in the gentlest, most unassuming way.

Even when life threw her a curveball—a fall, a fracture, a cast—Brooke rarely complained. Instead, she found ways to stay connected and involved, cheering others on, offering encouragement, and letting her spirit lead the way.

And when she had news to share, it was an event in itself. I'll never forget the time she was trying to tell us something big and her whole face lit up with anticipation as she slowly, patiently guided us toward understanding. After a few back-and-forth guesses, we finally got it: her sister had just had a baby! Her eyes gleamed with pride, and when we said the words out loud, her grin stretched ear to ear, as if the joy couldn't be contained.

That's who Brooke is: hopeful, loving, patient, endlessly expressive, and deeply connected to the people she loves. Today, she remains a beloved part of The Angelus family, a story still unfolding with laughter, connection, and quiet determination. And when I go back for a visit, Brooke reminds me that joy lives in the details, in a well-timed glance, a gentle tap, a quick shake of the head, and a smile that says, Yes, that's it. You got it.

MARY:
A LIFE OF JOY AND CELEBRATION

Mary arrived at The Angelus just as we were putting the finishing touches on our first home in Hudson. Her new bedroom was decorated with wallpaper that shimmered—delicate flowers and butterflies dancing across the walls. It felt like a fresh start, not just for her, but for all of us. She was beaming. For the first time in a long time, Mary had a space of her own—a room filled with warmth and comfort— a far cry from the institutional dormitory she had known before. She was so proud of that room. Though she would eventually share it, those early days when it was just hers brought her a quiet happiness that was plain to see.

Mary, who was in her mid-thirties when she became part of our family, had lived a complicated life before coming to us. One of four children, she lost her twin at birth. And when she was very young, her mother was hospitalized, leaving her early years full of change and uncertainty. She didn't speak, but she communicated in her own clear way using vocal sounds to get her point across. She relied on others for mobility and care, but there were many things she could still do on her own: feeding herself, drinking from a cup (even if there was the occasional spill), and flashing the most joyful smile at the smallest pleasures.

She settled in quickly, forming sweet connections with the other residents. Mary especially loved sitting in her recliner, working intently on cross-stitch projects, her hands busy and her focus steady. Just a few days after she arrived, she got a roommate — Gloria — a kind, soft-spoken woman in her forties. Gloria had been waiting in St. Petersburg for the Hudson house to be completed. Her mother was gracious and visited often, which, to be honest, stirred up some jealousy in Mary. She didn't love sharing attention, and one day she let Gloria know it, yelling loud enough that I had to intervene. I sent her to her room like you would an upset child. I remember how she started wheezing, clearly worked up. I sat beside her and said gently but firmly, "That's not how we do things here." Then I stepped out and gave her a minute to calm down. And you know what? She did calm down. And as surprising as it sounds, that was the last time she ever had an episode like that. Something in her shifted. Maybe it was trust. Maybe it was knowing she was safe. Maybe it was just love doing its work.

Mary's family stayed in her life, though from a bit of a distance. Her father and stepmother visited for Christmas and our annual picnic. Later, after her father passed, her brother and sister took over, visiting with kindness and care. But in the past, when she was in the state institution, those visits were hard on her.

They stirred up so much emotion that she'd sometimes get sick afterward, even needing to be hospitalized a few times. That all changed once she found her rhythm with us. I truly believe the consistency, the acceptance, the feeling of being at home gave her the peace she'd always needed. And you could see it on her face during those family visits. Instead of fear or stress, there was calm. There was joy.

Mary flourished at The Angelus. She took part in our Adult Day Program with such enthusiasm, especially during arts and crafts. Her cross-stitching improved so much, and she was proud of every finished piece. But Mary wasn't just about the quiet moments. She had a big, bold love for entertainment. Country music, wrestling matches, you name it. She clapped and stomped along at Charlie Daniels concerts and cheered with gusto at wrestling events, giving a playful scowl to any wrestler playing the villain. One time, a wrestler came right over and shook her hand. You'd have thought she won a trophy.

And then there was Julio Iglesias. I'll never forget the look on her face when he stepped down from the stage, handed her a rose, and hugged her. That moment lit her up from the inside out and she carried that story with her like a treasure.

But if there was one thing Mary loved more than music or wrestling, it was birthdays. Oh, how she loved a birthday, especially her own. Her Seventieth was a year-long production, the event of the decade. She made a notebook full of ideas: the guest list, the menu, the decorations. She even wrote her invitations, handpicking each recipient with care. And of course, she selected the perfect cake and picked out her outfits. She planned every detail. Whether or not she truly wanted it to be a surprise is anyone's guess. Knowing Mary, it was easy for me to imagine that the idea of a surprise party struck her as delightfully dramatic and perfectly fitting for such a milestone.

When the big day arrived, more than fifty guests—board members, staff, longtime friends—filled the decorated cafeteria, waiting quietly before shouting, "Surprise!" as Mary entered. Overcome with emotion, Mary burst into tears of joy, especially when she spotted her brother and sister among the crowd. She stood there, beaming through happy tears, taking in the laughter, the love, and the warmth that surrounded her. And with her signature grace and gratitude, she thanked everyone—sincerely and from the heart—for a celebration she had dreamed of, and in her own special way, helped bring to life.

As the years have gone by, Mary has slowed down. She's earned it. She still likes to pick out just the right outfit for the day (and remind everyone she picked it), enjoy her favorite snacks, and looks forward to bedtime the way others look forward to a night out on the town, cozying up with the same deep contentment she once felt after a full day of crafting, cheering, or laughing at a party. She still gets a little cranky when things don't go her way, but even then, there's a twinkle behind the frown. That spark is still there, reminding us she's watching, she has opinions, and she expects to be heard.

But the most extraordinary thing about Mary's life isn't just that, since coming to The Angelus, she has never once needed to be hospitalized, it's how deeply she's been loved. The friendships, the routines, the music, and the laughter became the quiet foundation of her well-being. The Angelus didn't just give her a place to live. It gave her a place to shine. A place where birthdays became legendary, where musicians stepped off stage just for her, and where visitors knew her name before she ever had to tell them.

These days, I'm no longer there every morning like I used to be. I've stepped back, trusting the next generation to carry the torch. But I think about Mary often. I picture her, settled in her recliner with a snack in hand, maybe cross-stitching or picking out her outfit for the day, still very much herself, still reminding everyone who's boss. And I realize, in some small way, we helped build a life where she could feel safe, celebrated, and most of all, seen. That's what I had hoped for. And knowing she's still there, in the place she calls home, that's a comfort I carry with me every single day.

GLORIA:
A LIFE OF GRACE,
GIGGLES, AND GREAT BIG HUGS

I first met Gloria at one of Judy Stouffer's early wine-tasting fundraisers, held at a grand hotel near the beach. Gloria arrived with her
elderly mother, a gentle woman with kind eyes, who had cared for her
daughter faithfully since the day she was born. Gloria, though non-
verbal and using a wheelchair, needed no words to make an impression.
With just a glance, a nod, or the perfectly timed lift of her eyebrows,
she joined conversations in her own way and often stole the spotlight.
Her laughter, so warm and responsive, came exactly when the room
needed it most. She had a way of making people feel like they were in
on the same joke.

After the event, her mother pulled me aside. She was practical,
loving, and honest. "I won't be here forever," she said, and my heart
softened. It's a moment I've experienced with so many parents; the
knowing look, the quiet ache of responsibility. Gloria was her heart,
and she wanted to make sure her daughter would be safe and cared for
long after she was gone. Gloria had two married sisters, both with busy
lives and growing families, and while they loved her, they weren't in a
position to take on full-time care. So, we added Gloria to the waiting
list for our new house in Hudson, still under construction at the time.

When the home was ready, Gloria made the move, and her mother
came to help her settle in. There was something so touching about that

day; the way Gloria looked around her new room with wide eyes, and the way her mother tucked a few final things into drawers like she was folding down the corners of a love letter. It was a quiet handoff—heartbreaking and beautiful—and one I'll never forget.

Gloria fit in right away. She loved the meals, made fast friends with the staff, and took a particular liking to my husband, Dave. The two of them shared a special bond, not loud or showy, but easy and sweet. Most afternoons, I'd find them together on the front porch swing. Dave would have his arm around her, steadying the rhythm. While Gloria leaned back just slightly, catching the breeze. I'd step outside, hands on my hips, and tease, "All right, what's going on here?" Gloria would grin and shake her head, the picture of innocence, while Dave chuckled beside her. It became a daily ritual that brought smiles to all of us, every single time.

Her love for swings went way back. When she was a child, her father — a creative soul and a devoted dad—built her custom swings, little wagons, and even a carousel. He made magic for her. After his passing, her mother took over that role, doing her best to keep life rich, joyful, and full. But like many families, it wasn't always easy. Gloria's sisters sometimes struggled with the way attention and resources revolved around her, and that dynamic left its mark. That's the part of these stories we don't always talk about—the strain, the guilt, the balancing act—but it's real. And in Gloria's case, it was handled with quiet courage, even when it wasn't perfect.

Gloria's time with us was filled with joy and laughter. Her ability to understand and engage with those around her brought light to every corner of The Angelus, and her memory remains a beloved part of our history. She taught us about the importance of creating a home where everyone, regardless of their abilities, could find love, laughter, and belonging. Gloria gave so much to The Angelus. Her presence had a way of making people slow down and really listen—not just with their ears, but with their hearts. She understood far more than most people assumed, and she never missed a beat. Whether she was nodding along to a joke, lighting up at a visitor's hello, or sharing a knowing look with her favorite staff member, she brought joy wherever she went. Though she's no longer with us, Gloria remains one of the bright lights in our history—a reminder of how a person can speak volumes without ever saying a word. She taught us about connection, about gentleness, about the deep need we all have to belong somewhere. And she helped shape the kind of home The Angelus became.

Now, in retirement, I sometimes find myself thinking back to those porch swing moments: The laughter, the teasing, the way the breeze would lift the hem of Gloria's skirt as she smiled at Dave like they were sharing a secret. I may no longer be at The Angelus every day, but memories like that: They stay with you. They become part of who you are. Gloria left her mark on all of us. And for that, I'll always be grateful.

CHARLES:
A LEGACY OF FAMILY,
GENEROSITY, AND STRENGTH

Charles came to The Angelus from St. Petersburg, where he lived with his devoted parents and two loving sisters. Their home was just a few blocks from our old house on Castile Way, and their roots in the community ran deep. His grandfather, a dedicated member of the local Optimist Club, was a tireless advocate, not just for Charles, but for what he believed we were building at The Angelus.

At a luncheon where I had been invited to speak, his grandfather stood to share a few words. I still remember the way his voice cracked, eyes shimmering with tears, as he spoke about his grandson. Charles was blind, used a wheelchair, and didn't speak, and his body was often challenged by unpredictable movements and medical complexities. But what came through loudest was love—deep, unwavering love—and a grandfather's quiet prayer that his grandson would always be safe, cared for, and cherished.

That day marked the beginning of a remarkable partnership. Charles's grandfather became one of our most devoted champions. He planted the first trees along our driveway. He worked with his civic club to fund the six-foot fence around the backyard, and he showed up time and again to help however he could. You could feel his love for Charles in every nail hammered, every seed sown. His legacy is still here, planted deep in the soil of this place.

Charles's parents adored him. But like many families, they struggled with the decision to place their son in a group home. His youngest sister, especially, was fiercely protective. She worried about what life would be like for him away from the family. It was an emotional process, filled with questions and difficult conversations, but always, always, with Charles's best interests at heart.

When The Angelus relocated to Hudson, their support never wavered. Charles's grandfather and father personally installed a full sprinkler system across the ten-acre property. They planted magnolia trees as beautiful and strong as the love they carried for Charles. Eventually, after much thought and a great deal of trust, his parents decided to bring him to The Angelus.

We did what we could to honor that transition. His youngest sister helped decorate his bedroom, choosing colors and details she thought he'd like. It was a small gesture, but a meaningful one. It gave her a way to stay connected, to keep caring for her brother even as his world expanded.

At first, Charles's mother was understandably nervous. I don't think any parent ever stops wondering how their child is doing, no matter how old they are or how good the care might be. But slowly, she began to see that this new chapter could be a good one. She remained closely involved, joining me for his medical appointments, asking thoughtful questions, and making sure every detail of his care was right. Over time, her compassion reached even further. She became a legal guardian for several other children at The Angelus, kids who didn't have families of their own. Her heart just had that much room.

In those early years, Charles would often go home on weekends. But the transitions were hard on him. His mother noticed it too, and eventually, she made the incredibly selfless decision to let him stay full-time. That consistency helped him flourish. His family continued to visit often, bringing both sets of grandparents for holidays, picnics, and just because. He still faced medical challenges, but they came less frequently, and his days took on a peaceful rhythm. Surrounded by people who knew and loved him, Charles began to thrive.

As time went on, his sisters grew into strong, capable women. They married, had children of their own, but they never stopped showing up for their brother. Their love for him was steady, deep, and rooted in a lifetime of shared understanding. And Charles, for his part, became a quiet anchor within our home. He didn't need words to be known.

Charles passed away at the age of forty. It's hard to explain what his absence felt like, or how deeply he is missed. But his legacy lives on, not only in our memories, but in the very landscape of this place. The magnolia trees his family planted bloom each spring, their blossoms wide and fragrant, offering shade to the same walkways he once traveled.

ANDREW:
A JOURNEY OF RESILIENCE AND JOY

Andrew arrived at The Angelus when he was just six years old; a small boy with big, searching eyes and a quiet kind of determination. From the beginning, he needed a little extra care. His body was sensitive to strong smells, and even something as ordinary as the fumes from a school bus required careful planning. He didn't speak, but he communicated beautifully in other ways, through the gentlest smile, a curious tilt of the head, and a spirit that quietly invited you into his world.

What stood out most in those early days was how brave he was. Though his medical needs were many, and the road ahead was far from simple, Andrew faced each moment with remarkable resilience. At one point, his diet had to be strictly monitored, and later, he needed support with his nutrition in a more clinical way. That meant frequent trips back and forth to St. Petersburg for care, and our team did all we could to ensure that everything—from medications to mealtimes—was handled with precision and love.

His mother was a steady presence. Juggling the needs of three other boys, her job, and her deep devotion to Andrew, she made it look easier than it was. We worked closely together to make things manageable for the whole family. During the week, Andrew stayed at The Angelus and attended a nearby school. On weekends, he went home; a rhythm that allowed him to be part of both worlds.

He also formed a close bond with his stepfather, who embraced Andrew like his own son. Their connection was quiet but real; the kind that speaks louder than words.

But life doesn't always follow a plan. Andrew's mother made the brave decision to enlist in the military, which brought both pride and new challenges. While she was away, Andrew's stepfather did his best to hold everything together, but over time, the weight of it all began to show. The family's dynamic shifted. Things changed. And when his mom returned home, she carried both strength and invisible scars from her service. She later received a military disability, and although that chapter came with its own difficulties, it didn't stop her from beginning again. When she remarried, Andrew was there, dressed for the occasion, beaming with pride, embracing his new stepfather with open arms. I can still picture his smile that day. He was so proud to be part of it.

This new stepfather, moved by Andrew's heart and by what he saw at The Angelus, became one of our generous supporters for years—a quiet gesture that spoke volumes about the impact Andrew had on those who knew him.

Then, Andrew's mother passed away. It was sudden and left many questions unanswered. But one thing was never in doubt: Andrew loved his mother deeply. And though he never spoke it aloud, you could see it in his eyes every time her name came up, that quiet flicker of memory, of something sacred held close.

Today, Andrew's world is steady and full. He still lives at Booth House, alongside housemates who have become more like family, some of whom have shared his home for over thirty years. In the Day Program, he moves through his routines with quiet curiosity, always taking everything in with that same warm smile that first captured our hearts. He's healthy, stable, and well cared for, surrounded by people who know his rhythms and honor his needs.

Holidays are especially joyful. His brothers, now grown, tall, bearded, and proud, never missed a Thanksgiving or Christmas brunch.

They tower over him now, but to Andrew, they are still his brothers. When they walk in, his face lights up. They sit beside him, crack jokes with the staff, and treat him with the same gentle, patient, and protective love they always have. You can feel the bond between them like a thread that's never frayed.

Andrew may not use words, but he speaks in all the ways that matter. In the twinkle of his eye. In the way he listens, in the calm, he carries into a room. He holds onto his memories of his mother, of his family, of the place he's called home for most of his life, and he continues to grow within that space, in quiet strength.

I don't see him every day anymore. But when I close my eyes and think of him, I still picture that same small boy with a brave spirit, and now, a man with a legacy of love around him. He has been part of our story for so long, and we are better for it.

GORDON:
A LIFE OF JOY,
PROGRESS, AND BELONGING

Gordon came into our lives at The Angelus one bright afternoon at our annual family picnic. He arrived with his devoted grandparents; kind, warm people who had raised him with care and consistency. Alongside them was his mother, a gentle woman who had done her very best, with the help of her parents, to provide Gordon the life he deserved. But as Gordon grew older and taller, the care he required became more than they could physically manage. They were looking for a place where he could be well cared for and be surrounded by others who honored who he was.

Though Gordon used a wheelchair and needed some help with transfers, he had an exuberance about him that couldn't be missed. He was able to speak, though his speech was sometimes difficult to understand, especially for those who didn't know him well. His hands were often clenched, making it tricky for him to grasp or hold items, but none of that ever dimmed his enthusiasm. The joy he felt seemed to bubble up and could not be contained. His personality—bright, funny, and full of life—came through in everything he did.

After a long wait filled with paperwork and phone calls, and caseworkers, Gordon finally joined our home at The Angelus. And from the moment he moved in, everything began to shift for him and his family. His mother came to visit each weekend, happy to see her son settling into his new house and community. It was during one of her visits that I discovered something unexpected. I had gone to grade school with Gordon's aunt in St. Petersburg. It was a small detail, but one that made the world feel comfortingly close-knit and added another layer to the connection between our families.

Gordon quickly became one of our bright lights. He absolutely loved the swimming pool. The water gave him a kind of freedom that's hard to describe, as if all the things that challenged him on land just didn't exist in the water. He'd push himself under and pop back up with a triumphant, "Watch this!" like he was performing for an adoring audience, and in truth, he was. His joy in the pool was infectious, and we never tired of cheering him on.

As time went on, Gordon kept learning. With the support of tools designed just for him (like adapted utensils and custom cups), he learned how to feed himself. It was slow at first, but he kept at it, building strength and confidence. He graduated from his school program with great pride and later moved into our adult day program, where his determination never waned.

He learned to use a stander, practiced with a walker, and improved his ability to wheel his own chair across the room. And when did he figure out how to ride a tricycle? You would've thought he won the Tour de France. It's still one of his favorite things to do, pedaling proudly, laughing as he rides.

Over the years, Gordon experienced a heartbreaking loss. His mother and grandparents, who had stood beside him for so long, eventually passed. But the love they poured into him never left. It continues through the friendships he's built at The Angelus and in the way the staff and residents show up for him every day, like family.

Today, Gordon is a grown man with a laugh you can hear from across the room. He jokes with staff, lights up at parties, and participates in just about everything with joy and purpose. He brings people together without even trying. His happiness is the kind that reaches you, the kind that stays with you long after you've left the room.

Now, decades after his first day here, Gordon's story reminds me why we started The Angelus in the first place. He is living proof of what a loving, supportive environment can do. His journey is one of growth and grit, of everyday triumphs that add up to an extraordinary life. When I think of Gordon—and I often do—I picture him in the pool, surfacing with that triumphant grin, shouting "Watch this!" as if the world were his stage. And honestly, it is.

ANN AHERN:
A LEGACY OF FAITH AND DEVOTION

Ann first connected with The Angelus in 1981, drawn by a deep understanding of the unique challenges faced by children with disabilities. Like many of our residents, Ann had physical limitations as she used a power wheelchair and communicated with effort, but her life was a shining example of perseverance. Despite the barriers she faced, Ann lived independently in her own home with the help of around-the-clock caregivers. Her father, a determined attorney, made sure she received a college education. Over eight years, Ann earned her degree in education, a tremendous achievement. Yet despite her qualifications, her speech was difficult for many to understand, which made finding a teaching position nearly impossible. Still, Ann's spirit never wavered.

I'll never forget her first visit to The Angelus. She lit up as she communicated with one of our residents using a communication board. The two of them carried on a joyful exchange, full of laughter and understanding. That moment solidified Ann's belief that access and connection should never be considered luxuries. She left inspired, and, in true Ann fashion, she took action.

Shortly after that visit, she organized a Valentine's Dinner fundraiser to help us purchase a desperately needed van with a wheelchair lift. Thanks to her tenacity and the generosity of donors like Lowell Paxson and Jack Staples, The Angelus received a used Ford van with a Braun lift. That van changed everything as it brought freedom and possibility to our community.

As the years passed, Ann became more than a supporter. She became part of our family. But even as she gave so much to others, her own world was shaken. It was discovered that her caregivers had been stealing from her, leaving her bank account drained and her future uncertain. It was a betrayal that would have devastated most people. But Ann, with the guidance of her attorney, chose hope. She sold her home in St. Petersburg and made plans to build a new one right here on The Angelus property, where she would be safe, supported, and surrounded by people who cared.

We offered her a small parcel of land near Booth House, and Ann eagerly began designing her dream home; a modest, yet comfortable two-bedroom, one-bathroom house with a screened back porch and a carport for her van. But just as construction plans were underway, we hit a snag. A state regulation had recently been passed that restricted group homes for individuals with developmental disabilities from being located within 1,000 feet of each other. It threatened not just Ann's home, but the vision we had for future expansion.

Determined to find a solution, I reached out to Steve Booth, our attorney and longtime ally. Thankfully, I had previously purchased several acres of land next to The Angelus, originally intended for my children. I transferred one of those acres to The Angelus, which placed Ann's home just far enough away to meet the regulation. By 1991, the home was complete. We called it Ann House, and it stood as a symbol of her perseverance, generosity, and what community can truly mean.

In her new home, Ann thrived. She found a renewed sense of purpose, working in the day program's computer class, where she helped students use adaptive technology. Under Dave's guidance, instructional software was developed to meet each resident's unique abilities. Ann had a gift for knowing when someone needed help and how to offer it gently. She taught with her eyes and her patience, guiding others through technology with quiet encouragement.

We took special care in selecting Ann's caregivers, ensuring that she received not only reliable support but also the respect and dignity she deserved. While she required assistance with certain daily tasks, she maintained her independence, feeding herself and enjoying meals with staff and friends. Surrounded by a community that valued her contributions, Ann was happy, fulfilled, and truly at home.

When Ann passed away in 1993, we were heartbroken. But in true Ann fashion, her final act was one of generosity. She left her home for The Angelus, ensuring that her legacy would continue. We renovated the space, adding more bedrooms, bathrooms, and a common area. Ann House became our third residential home, a warm, lively space filled with laughter, music, and friendship.

Today, it's home to six wonderful individuals, each with their own spark, their own stories, and their own way of carrying forward Ann's legacy. A plaque on the front door honors her name, but her true legacy lives in every conversation around the dinner table, every shared celebration, every act of care that happens under that roof.

Ann wasn't just a donor. She was a teacher, a neighbor, and a daily presence in our lives. Though her voice was hard to understand, her message was always clear: we all have something to give. And she gave what she could every day. She gave her time, her trust, her home, and her heart.

Every time I walk by Ann House and hear the laughter inside, I smile. Ann House remains exactly what she hoped it would be, not just a building, but a promise kept.

GRANT:
A LIFE OF RESILIENCE AND COMMUNITY

When I first met Grant, he was living at home with his elderly father in a modest, well-kept house. I'll never forget the sight of him, smiling, steady, pedaling away on a stationary bike. His leg braces moved rhythmically, helping him stay active and strong. Though he faced physical challenges from an illness in childhood, his spirit was anything but limited. His parents had made sure he went to school, where he developed a deep love of reading. His hands weren't able to hold a pencil, but he adapted with special tools, learning how to feed himself, and finger foods were his favorite, of course.

As I sat at their kitchen table explaining our Angelus Day Program, both father and son leaned in, full of interest. Within just a few weeks, Grant was on the STAR bus each morning, often riding alongside Walter and Norman, two brothers who would become his closest friends. Though he couldn't walk, he transferred with ease, and he quickly became a vibrant part of our Angelus community.

Grant participated in every class we offered. He was eager to learn, always asking questions, always ready to try. Dave even created a custom computer game just for him, using a switch mounted beside the keyboard. Grant mastered it quickly, then challenged Dave to make it harder! His favorite class, though, was always kitchen skills. I suspect it had less to do with the cooking and more to do with the volunteer who taught it. Every afternoon, Grant made sure she said goodbye before he boarded the bus. It was their little ritual, simple, sweet, and full of meaning.

Socially, Grant blossomed. He had a natural way of making people feel comfortable. Walter and Norman understood him effortlessly, and even Mara who communicated in her own expressive way did her best to join their conversations. Mornings often began with music class, and it didn't take much to fill the room: Lou would come out of her office, Dave would leave the computer lab, and Debbie would arrive with the gardening crew. Soon, the space was alive with the sound of maracas, bells, cymbals, offbeat singing, and joyful noise. Everyone, no matter how they communicated, joined in for our favorite chorus of "God Bless America." It was messy and beautiful, and entirely ours.

By 1992, when our third residence was completed, Grant's father's health had declined, and he knew it was time for a change. He wanted to move to an assisted living facility, but only after ensuring Grant was in a safe, supportive place surrounded by familiar faces. When Grant moved into the Angelus, he embraced his new home wholeheartedly, strengthening his friendships and settling into the rhythms of community life.

Around that time, Grant's sister, who lived in Chicago, invited him to visit. It was a thrilling opportunity, and she generously arranged for Dave and me to accompany him. She even booked us a hotel on the Magnificent Mile. My son Joe, who worked for Continental Airlines, helped with the travel arrangements, and Pete came along for the adventure, eager to see the city of his sports heroes: the Bears, the White Sox, and of course, Michael Jordan's Bulls.

Chicago didn't disappoint. While Grant spent a joyful weekend with his sister and brother-in-law (who, funnily enough, was also named Grant), the rest of us explored the city. We rode a boat through downtown, visited Navy Pier, and marveled at the views from the giant Ferris wheel. Pete and Dave rode to the top together while I waved from the ground. We even toured a baseball bat factory where Pete picked out a souvenir he was enormously proud of. It was a trip full of laughter, discovery, and connection with the kind of memories that become part of who you are.

Eventually, Grant's sister moved closer, settling in a city not too far from The Angelus, and began visiting nearly every weekend. Their bond remained strong, although her visits came with a touch of sisterly accountability. Grant loved a good meal, and she kept a watchful eye on his diet. After a restaurant outing, he'd sometimes return shaking his head with a grin, "She wouldn't let me have mashed potatoes or french fries!" It always made us laugh.

Through every change and challenge, Grant remained steady, kind, quick-witted, and endlessly thoughtful. He was deeply connected to the people around him. His life is a testament to what's possible when someone is truly seen, supported, and loved.

I think of Grant often. I picture him at the kitchen table with his friends, teasing the staff with a clever joke, or turning to wave goodbye before boarding the bus. Grant didn't just find a home at The Angelus; he helped make it one. And anyone who had the gift of knowing him would say the same: he gave just as much love as he received, and then some.

JACK:
THE ANGELUS SPOKESMAN
WITH A HEART OF GOLD

Jack arrived at The Angelus in 1993, the final addition to the "Bachelor Pad" at Ann House, and brought with him an irresistible charm, quick wit, and a spirit that refused to be diminished by anything life had thrown at him. His journey there began with a quiet hero: Uncle Eddie, who stepped in when Jack's future was hanging in the balance.

Jack had lived an active and social life in another state where he was mainstreamed in school, made many friends, and never met a stranger. But after his mother passed away, things took a complicated turn. He was relocated to Florida to live with Uncle Ike and Aunt Bea, kind, elderly relatives who loved him deeply but weren't equipped for the day-to-day care he required. The move was sudden, and in the shuffle, his wheelchair was left behind.

But Jack, being Jack, he made the best of it. He told me stories about how he'd kneel on the floor to eat, trying to outmaneuver their playful dog. "That dog had good taste," he said, grinning. "I was just faster." Most people would've told that story with frustration. Jack told it with laughter. That was his gift: patience, practicality, and a sense of humor that never wavered.

He scooted around the house on his knees, answering the phone, helping where he could, and insisting to friends who called, "Oh, I'm just fine." He didn't even know the water had been shut off until one day it simply didn't come on. He just smiled when he told me about it. No drama, just another story from life's parade.

Uncle Ike may have been showing signs of memory loss, but whether it was that or simply their shared "it'll be fine" attitude, Jack always remained calm. Uncle Ike liked to take Jack on fishing trips, an adventure they both really loved, even though there wasn't a wheelchair and no safe transport options. The solution? Jack simply lay in the back seat of the car and then scooted with his fishing pole down to the lake. One time, Uncle Ike got lost on the way home and started to panic. Jack, calm as ever, lying down in the back seat, reassured him,

"Don't worry, Uncle Ike. You'll find it."

With concern for Uncle Ike and Aunt Bea's health, and for Jack's well-being, Uncle Eddie stepped in and changed Jack's life. Uncle Eddie arranged to take Jack to see a new place that could be his new home. And just like that, Jack found himself once again lying down in the backseat of a car, this time Uncle Eddie's car, on his way to a place called The Angelus. Jack's arrival was as grand as the life he would go on to build here. Grinning from the backseat of Uncle Eddie's car, Jack called out as he rolled into the driveway of Ann House:

"Honey, I'm home!" And he was, in every way.

From day one, Jack was a gentleman, a jokester, and a friend. Uncle Eddie remained his biggest supporter, visiting often with wristwatches for the guys, special treats, and farm-fresh corn from Tavares, small reminders that Jack was deeply loved and never forgotten. Eddie's well-trained border collie, Winnie, always accompanied him and brought joy to the household, greeting everyone with wet kisses.

Jack was fitted for a custom-molded wheelchair that gave him the support and freedom to explore every corner of the property. And explore he did, while always finding ways to be useful: delivering mail, helping feed the horses and goats by pulling a wagon behind his chair loaded with hay and grain. These weren't chores to Jack. They were expressions of purpose, pride, and joy.

I think of Jack as the unofficial spokesman. He doesn't just talk about The Angelus; he lives it. He shares his love for his Angelus community freely, greeting guests, answering questions, and welcoming new residents with ease and warmth. His presence is steady, dependable, and full of cheerfulness, saying, "I love this place." And you knew he meant it.

Jack's love of racing runs deep. He's a die-hard NASCAR fan, and one of the greatest moments of his life was attending the Daytona 500 with Dave and Joe, where he met Richard Petty, his absolute hero. He's retold that story hundreds of times, each version just as animated as the last. Jack also founded "The Angelus Mile," a wheelchair race he trained for with such determination that he wore out two sets of tires before race day even arrived. He didn't need to win, he already knew he was a champion.

My son Marty was a dirt race car driver, and we often took the residents to races, complete with a BBQ for a picnic. One time, Joe brought a bus load of residents to the track, and they lifted Jack, Sam, and Pete into the driver's seat for short spins. A thrill of a lifetime!!! He loved racing so much that one time, when we went to watch my grandson race at a karting track, he asked the owner if he could "run the track." During the lunch break, Jack was allowed on the track, with my grandson riding a bicycle alongside him. By the end, his hands were blistered, but he was grinning ear to ear.

Jack never forgets his roots. One year, Dave and I took him on a road trip back to his hometown so he could reconnect with old classmates. The reunion was full of laughter, storytelling, and long hugs. He even visited his best friend's grave, blowing a kiss to the sky as he always does when remembering someone he loves. That trip wasn't a goodbye; it was a bridge between where he came from and where he belongs now.

Today, Jack is still one of the most active, cheerful, and involved people I know. He keeps his room tidy, writes me letters often, and offers advice—sometimes solicited, sometimes not—to staff and residents alike. He's still watching every race, still delivering joy on wheels, still reminding everyone around him that life is meant to be lived fully.

And if you're lucky enough to visit The Angelus, you'll hear him before you see him; his voice full of mischief and welcome, calling out one of his two favorite phrases, "Honey, I'm home!" or "Drivers, start your engines!"

THE CHRISTMAS PAGEANT:
A LIVING NATIVITY

By 1990, all the houses at The Angelus were completed and filled with residents. With Christmas approaching, I wanted to create something magical, a pageant that would bring the spirit of the holiday to life while allowing our residents to take center stage. Inspired by the true story of Christmas, I wrote a narrative featuring the angel Gabriel, the three wise men, and, of course, the stable in Bethlehem.

Dave, who had a rich and commanding voice, became the narrator. He practiced tirelessly, using a microphone and recording equipment to perfect his delivery. Meanwhile, I was busy sewing costumes, designing oversized garments that fit comfortably over wheelchairs. Perri contributed her artistic talents, cutting out and painting two enormous plywood camels and two larger-than-life angels. Together, Dave and Jerry worked on setting up the lights, coordinating them with the music and the narrative to create an immersive experience.

The Christmas Pageant was designed as a "walking pageant," where spectators would follow the story as they moved along the sidewalks. Dave controlled the sound system from a van parked near the horse pens, while the staff guided the crowd and helped with transitions.

Mara played the angel Gabriel, and Sam walked beside her, holding onto the back of his wheelchair for support. As the procession moved along, spectators passed by the camels and the three wise men. The characters sometimes changed depending on the weather or if a resident was unwell, but everyone took their roles seriously. A drummer boy joined the journey to the beat of "Rum Pa Pum Pum," and more scenes were added over time: a village, a blacksmith shop, and eventually the stable.

At the stable, Baby Jesus (played by Jamie), Mary (Mary), and Joseph (Jack) were joined by wooden cows, creating a serene nativity scene. A large star marked the journey's end, and the group sang "Silent Night" as staff distributed candles to the spectators, who joined in the song.

The finale was breathtaking: a group of angels in white gowns with red bows appeared before a big blue wall near the red barn. Pete, dressed in a bright red blazer, conducted the "choir of angels" in the "Hallelujah Chorus." All the residents joined for the final number, their wheelchairs carefully positioned by staff hiding among the trees.

The Christmas Pageant ended with spectators pushing residents to the Day Program building for cookies and hot chocolate, bringing a warm sense of community to the evening.

The tradition continued for more than twenty years. When Charlie Daniels attended for one year, he was so impressed that he offered to narrate the program himself. His professional narration and sound equipment elevated the production, though even Dave, our original narrator, agreed it was a wonderful change.

As the years went on, my granddaughter Joelle became an integral part of the pageant. She initially (about 10 years old at the time) led a miniature horse alongside the angel Gabriel, managing the mischievous animal's playful nips while trying to keep him on track. As she got older, Joelle took on more responsibility, operating the lights and narration tapes from a new set Dave created for her, appropriately called "the Inn."

The pageant was more than a performance; it was a community celebration. Local churches joined us, singing carols and even bringing a bell choir. The Christmas cards made by the residents in their arts and crafts classes were always in demand at the pageant "merch" table.

For more than two decades, the Christmas Pageant truly brought the *magic of a child, the magic of Christmas.* Words that also appeared on the cover of our annual holiday card.

And it truly did, not just with lights and costumes, but with something deeper. It gave our residents the spotlight, not for what they couldn't do, but for all that they could. They became angels and wise men, shepherds, and innkeepers, and for a little while each December, they showed the world what it means to lead with love. I carry those memories with so much pride: the songs, the lights, the cold air and warm cocoa, the sight of families gathered shoulder to shoulder, watching our residents shine. And yet, I'll admit, it still aches a little to think of the final years when the crowd thinned, and the music echoed into quieter nights. Letting it go was hard. But even now, I can close my eyes and see it all: Pete in his red blazer, the camels Perri painted, Joelle leading the miniature horse through the dark. It lives in me still, that pageant. A gift we gave the world, and one I'll never forget.

WALTER & NORMAN:
A BROTHERHOOD
OF JOY AND ADVENTURE

Walter and Norman were more than just brothers; they were an inseparable duo, bound by love, humor, and a shared sense of adventure. When they joined The Angelus's newly formed school, they were already well into adulthood—Walter and Norman—living at home with their devoted eighty-year-old mother. Though both men used wheelchairs, they propelled themselves independently, bringing an energy and vibrancy that made them instantly beloved members of the community.

The brothers were as self-sufficient as they were charismatic. They fed themselves heartily, bringing homemade lunches packed by their mother, which often included pork chops, sometimes even with the bone still in, or pork chop sandwiches. Walter, the more talkative of the two, had a gruff accent and an opinion on just about everything, while Norman, the quieter brother, spoke with hesitation but always had something thoughtful to say. Walter also took charge of their cigarettes, rationing them to Norman as he saw fit, and carried Tic-Tacs in his pocket, perhaps as a post-smoke breath freshener, perhaps just because he liked them.

At first, Walter and Norman arrived at school using city transportation, a service that also brought other disabled adults like Grant, Bill, and Rose. But when city funding for the service ended, The Angelus stepped in, using its van to ensure no one was left behind. It was a long road, securing transportation funding, hiring drivers, covering fuel and insurance, but in the end, it was worth every effort to keep Walter, Norman, and their friends connected to their community.

As their mother aged and could no longer care for them, Walter and Norman made the transition to living at The Angelus. They settled into their new home with remarkable ease, even giving up smoking without complaint to comply with house rules. They moved into the third residence alongside Jack, Don, Grant, and Travis, forming a lively group of men who quickly became like family. With The Angelus's big van, complete with a lift and tie-downs, the brothers were able to embark on adventures they had never imagined.

One of their most unforgettable experiences was a two-day trip to Disney World, where they stayed at the Disney campground, soaking in the magic like kids on their first visit. But that was just the beginning. Walter and Norman became regulars at fishing trips, bowling outings, wrestling matches, Buccaneers football games, and, of course, Charlie Daniels concerts. If there was an event, they were there, ready to soak up every moment.

Their enthusiasm was contagious. At annual picnics, they were the heart of the square-dancing team, twirling their chairs with joy and laughter. They attended concerts, never missed a church service, and relished every fishing trip. Their mother, a steadfast presence in their lives, visited often, deeply grateful for the happiness and care her sons received.

After her passing, Walter and Norman remained at The Angelus for another fifteen years, continuing to fill their days with adventure and companionship. When their health declined, they transitioned to a nursing home, but their spirit never faded. We visited often, making sure they had their radios and CD players.

Walter and Norman's journey is a testament to the power of love, adventure, and the impact of a supportive community. Their time at The Angelus gave them opportunities they had never known, but more importantly, it gave them a home filled with friendship, laughter, and the freedom to experience life to the fullest. Their story is not just one of resilience; it's a reminder that joy, when shared, becomes a legacy that never fades.

BILL:
A GENTLE SOUL WHO
FOUND COMFORT IN A NEW HOME

Bill came to The Angelus thanks to a thoughtful referral from our dentist's secretary, Michelle, who had grown concerned about the challenges Bill's elderly mother was facing. At eighty years old, she was still lifting her tall, blind son, then in his early twenties, into a wheelchair to bring him to appointments. Her love and devotion were evident, but it was becoming more than she could physically manage. When we introduced her to the support The Angelus could provide, including transportation to our new Adult Day Training (ADT) program, she felt a deep sense of relief. Grateful for the opportunity, she applied for services, and Bill soon became one of our very first participants.

Bill was non-ambulatory and mostly non-verbal, though he could express himself through short, meaningful phrases. He also experienced muscle spasms, which required ongoing monitoring. His interests were simple and soothing; he loved to sit on the floor and flip through magazines, and music was his greatest joy. One of his favorite things to say was, "Radio on," and it became a gentle mantra in the space he helped shape. He attended every class we offered, including gardening, and he especially loved the outdoors. The sunshine made him smile, and the sound of birds always prompted a round of delighted clapping.

After several months in the day program, his mother, reassured by how well he was adjusting requested that Bill become a full-time resident. When Ann House was completed, Bill moved in alongside familiar faces from the ADT program: Walter, Norman, and Grant. Later, they were joined by Don and Jack, and together their house became known as the "bachelor pad." The camaraderie between them created a warm, supportive environment where each resident had space to grow and simply be themselves. Bill continued to thrive, finding happiness in his routine and the calm vibe of the home he now shared with close companions. When his mother passed away two years later, it was a difficult and heartbreaking moment for all who had come to know their bond. And yet, Bill remained peaceful and steady, a reflection of the comfort and security he found in his surroundings.

He spent twenty years with us, bringing a quiet joy and soft presence to every day. Whether it was the hum of a radio, the touch of sunshine, or the rustle of magazine pages, Bill found beauty in life's smallest moments. When he passed away, it was not just a resident we lost, but a piece of our collective heart.

Staff and residents who remember him fondly still say, "Radio on," as if he's just in the next room. And in many ways, he is. Bill's memory lingers in the light, in the music, and in the peaceful corners where joy once quietly lived.

OWEN:
A QUIET SOUL
WHO FOUND REFUGE AND CARE

Owen came to The Angelus under extraordinary circumstances. In the late 1990s, his family reached out in search of a safe and supportive home for him. At the time, we were at full capacity and sadly unable to accommodate him. But not long after, a second call came; this time from a concerned relative. Owen's mother had become gravely ill, and a series of unexpected events had left their home uninhabitable. Owen, in a moment none of us will forget, had been rescued by first responders during severe flooding. Given the urgency of his situation, emergency approval was granted for Owen to be admitted to The Angelus. Shortly thereafter, his mother passed away.

With the help and advocacy of his extended family, Owen was eventually enrolled in the services he needed to make his new home at The Angelus permanent.

Owen faced significant physical challenges. He was of small stature, non-verbal, and non-ambulatory, with a spinal condition that required careful support. Though blind due to cataracts, he had a strong sense of self and could feed himself with confidence and mealtimes quickly became a favorite part of his day. He was also quite strong; he could stand for transfers and even take a few assisted steps, and once you were in arm's reach—especially if you were wearing jewelry—you learned just how strong his grip could be.

He wasn't one for socializing. Owen preferred solitude and made his boundaries clear, often with a well-placed pinch. But that never stopped the staff from making sure he was included. They read to him, spoke to him gently, and took him to music concerts and community events. He didn't always react in ways we expected, but he never resisted the care he received. We learned to see his silence not as detachment, but as a quiet form of trust.

When his last close family member passed away, Owen no longer had visitors. But by then, he was already deeply woven into the fabric of our community. The staff became his family, learning his rhythms, respecting his space, and making sure he was always seen, even when he chose not to engage.

Owen stayed with us for nineteen years. In that time, he taught us so much about patience, respect, and what it means to care without needing anything in return. When he passed away in 2017 after a sudden illness, it was quiet, peaceful, and surrounded by the same love that had held him all those years.

Even now, when I think of Owen, I'm reminded that not all connections look the same. Some people speak with their eyes or their hands, and some, like Owen, teach us by simply being present. His life was a quiet one, but it mattered deeply to all of us.

CHARLIE DANIELS:
REBEL WITH A CAUSE

Charlie Daniels, beloved country musician, songwriter, fiddler, and storyteller, was one of the kindest souls I've ever met. He had generously chosen The Angelus as his favorite charity, and every year, he brought his band down to Hudson for a weekend of unforgettable music and joy. Officially inducted into the Country Music Hall of Fame in 2016, Charlie loved all the things that truly matter: God, faith, family, and country. He was a great American in every sense of the word. His songs reflected his deep convictions, and he despised crooked politicians and child abusers equally. Charlie was a rabble-rouser and an apostle, bringing joy to people around the world for decades, including America's troops in war-torn countries. How blessed we were that he chose to be an ambassador for The Angelus for twenty-seven unforgettable years!

It all started in December 1993 when Charlie came to Florida for a benefit for Connie Mack, who was then a U.S. Senator. Charlie loved being in Florida that time of year as his band had fewer "gigs" during December, and the warmer weather was always a welcome change. He asked his agent to find a nonprofit organization nearby that didn't have "fat cats," as he put it. That search led him to us.

At the time, our Hudson Avenue location was far from glamorous. The road wasn't even paved, and everything was coated in a layer of white lime rock dust from passing cars. But none of that mattered to Charlie. His limousine, escorted by a representative from the sheriff's office, arrived at our newly constructed building. Inside, we had prepared a welcome prayer service and anxiously awaited the opportunity to meet this celebrity who had taken an interest in us. When the limo door opened, out stepped this giant of a man wearing a cowboy hat, and every single one of us—kids and staff alike—was starstruck.

Charlie and his wife, Hazel, walked through the prayer service aisle, taking the time to meet every single resident. Even our verbal residents were so awestruck they couldn't find the words to speak. But Charlie had a way of putting everyone at ease. He sang a few gospel songs before leading us in Christmas favorites like "Frosty the Snowman" and "Grandma Got Run Over by a Reindeer." Slowly but surely, everyone joined in, and the nervous energy transformed into pure joy. We served coffee, orange juice, and muffins as Charlie and Hazel mingled with the kids, their parents, and our staff, making everyone feel like they had known them forever.

That visit was the start of a beautiful friendship. Charlie and the board of directors formed a committee to create the annual Charlie Daniels Event, a fundraiser that ran for twenty-seven years. Charlie would bring his entire band, his massive tour bus, and a group of talented friends to perform. Over the years, we have had the pleasure of meeting Vince Gill, Tommy Cash, Toby Keith, Clint Black, The Marshall Tucker Band, Montgomery Gentry, Marilyn Sellars, The Hager Twins, Lucinda Crosby, and so many others. Even TV personalities like the Captains from *Deadliest Catch* and cartoonist Guy Gilchrist joined the festivities. Guy, in particular, became a regular visitor, delighting our kids by drawing cartoons on the tablecloths and singing for them.

The weekend events were always a whirlwind. Friday night kicked off with a pairing party, bringing together golfers with celebrities they would team up with for the tournament. Gar and Tammy Williams, our dedicated committee chairs, worked tirelessly to organize everything, including a preview of the silent auction items. Saturday morning began with a shotgun start at the golf course, where donors and celebrities enjoyed breakfast, lunch, and a day on the greens. Activities were planned for the golfers' wives, ranging from boat trips to fashion shows to luxurious luncheons with professional chefs.

Saturday night was the crown jewel of the weekend – the awards banquet. With six hundred guests in attendance, the evening was filled with laughter, music, and fundraising. A local radio announcer emceed the event, and Charlie often donated his cowboy hat to liven up the live auction. Celebrities mingled with the crowd, signing autographs, and the night ended with a performance from Charlie and his band. He always brought the house down with "The Devil Went Down to Georgia," often joined by other musicians in an impromptu jam session that stretched late into the night.

On Sunday morning, at 8:30 a.m., we held our prayer service at The Angelus. Charlie and Hazel greeted every resident, and by the second year, Charlie had memorized the names and personal stories of everyone. He'd ask Jack about NASCAR, hold Mary's hand during the service, and chat with Dave about sound equipment, even arranging for microphones or guitar stands to be delivered. The service always featured Charlie's powerful rendition of "How Great Thou Art," sometimes with other celebrity guests joining in. It was a deeply moving experience every single time.

After the service, everyone scrambled to get ready for the outdoor concert held in a nearby pasture. Volunteers set up a massive stage, parking lots, food vendors, and security, while residents and staff loaded onto buses to enjoy the show. It was a monumental effort, but the joy and unity it brought to everyone involved made it worth it.

A few years into the event, the Seminole Hard Rock Casino and Hotel became the primary venue for the celebrities and their families. The golfers purchased weekend packages, which included luxurious accommodations and exclusive access to nightly jam sessions. Mr. Fontana, the hotel manager, and his wife, Marilyn, became close friends of Charlie and Hazel. Both couples were deeply invested in The Angelus and its mission, and they marveled at how the event's success translated into tangible improvements for our residents.

By 1999, Charlie's unwavering support inspired a dream that had quietly taken root in my heart: I wanted to build a lodge. One afternoon, I asked our chairman of the board, Steve Booth, to walk with me through the wooded acres behind The Angelus. As we meandered down the quiet paths, I shared my vision of a summer camp for children with disabilities. A place where kids could come for a real vacation, and parents could rest easy knowing their loved ones were cared for in a nurturing environment. I could imagine families from all over the United States, perhaps escaping harsh northern winters and taking a much-needed vacation, knowing their child was safe, cared for, and having the time of their life enjoying the warmth of Florida. I envisioned campers swimming, brushing and feeding the miniature horses, making arts and crafts, gardening, learning computer skills, and even selecting a day trip to Busch Gardens, SeaWorld, or Disney. I had so many ideas! The first step in this dream was to build a lodge, which would be named "Charlie's Lodge" in his honor.

As Steve and I walked along the pathway on the property, I pointed out to Steve the future locations for small cabins tucked among the trees. Then, rounding a final curve, I stopped and gestured to a wide-open space where I imagined a grand log cabin—the main lodge. "It will be the heart of the camp," I said, "with a large gathering space for meals and activities." I brought pictures of log cabins that Dave and I had collected during a weekend trip to North Carolina. We'd been doing our homework. Steve was on board and volunteered to spearhead the project. He supported the idea of the camp and helping families, and he also saw the potential of a new source of revenue for The Angelus. "Yes," I said, "And we could run the camp year-round!"

True to form, Steve got the ball rolling. He formed a building committee made up of trusted members of the community. One of them, Dan Patterson, shared how he had built a church for the Jehovah's Witnesses using volunteers. That sparked something in all of us. After several planning sessions, we chose a log cabin company and redesigned the structure to fit our vision. Before any building could begin, we had to comply with Southwest Florida Water Management District requirements. That meant a massive retention pond had to be dug. My friend Fred Deuel's surveying company handled the land survey, and soon, trees came down and the land began to transform. A rep from the log company met with our team, and together we strategized.

We ordered the logs, cleared the site, and set up a work trailer. A long hand-washing trough was built for the crew, and volunteers started pouring in, mostly on weekends, since most had full-time jobs. Holes were drilled into the massive logs for the rods that would hold them together. One of our board members worked in the sheriff's office and was authorized to bring in a dozen inmates with construction experience, supervised by Mr. Chittum. Weekday progress picked up speed, thanks to their skilled hands and generous hearts.

Volunteers poured in from all over the community, including inmates from the sheriff's department who worked during the week. On some weekends, over sixty volunteers arrived to lend a hand. Women prepared hearty meals of chili, stews, homemade bread, and cookies for the workers, turning lunchtime into a celebration of camaraderie. Mealtimes were filled with laughter and stories.

The towering outer walls of the two-story lodge were first built flat on the ground, then lifted into place by a massive crane, graciously donated along with its operator. The moment that first wall rose was electric. Just as we held our breath watching it lift, a loud BANG rang out. Everyone froze. Thankfully, it wasn't the crane; it was a blown-out tire on the soda wagon! That sound gave us all a scare and a memory we'd never forget.

One local policeman, an expert carpenter, crafted a breathtaking symmetrical ceiling. A local tile company owner donated his time and materials, installing beautiful ceramic tiles with unique designs in each of the three bathrooms. To this day, I regret missing the opportunity to give him and his wife the special volunteer T-shirts we had made. It was an honest oversight, but one that still bothers me.

As the finishing touches were being made, one of our volunteers, Kurt, the marketing director at the local hospital took on the grand fireplace in the main lodge room. He picked out gorgeous stone from a local yard and painstakingly laid it, night after night after work, often staying as late as 9:00 p.m.. His wife would call, worried, and I'd tell her he was still up on the scaffolding, trying to finish in time for the opening.

On the very last night, with the grand opening looming, the scaffolding just wasn't high enough. Kurt rigged together a makeshift platform out of ten-gallon cans and somehow balanced himself high enough to place the final stones. He finished at 11:00 p.m.. Meanwhile, Jim Campbell was still installing the flooring. I don't know how late he stayed, maybe all night.

And then the day arrived. The lodge was finally ready in time for Charlie and Hazel's visit! Dave and Dan greeted Charlie and Hazel with a beautifully decorated horse-drawn buggy. As they trotted through the winding, wooded road, the trees parted to reveal the stunning log cabin, surrounded by cheering volunteers and residents. Everyone, residents, staff, and volunteers stood waiting, clapping, and cheering as the horses came to a stop under the portico. Over the door was a carved wooden sign that read: CHARLIE'S LODGE.

Charlie stepped out of the buggy, tears in his eyes. Many of us were crying, too. What we didn't know was that Charlie had laryngitis and was under doctor's orders not to speak or sing. Most performers would've canceled, but not Charlie. Instead, he quietly arranged for a dear friend to perform in his place at the concert. Even though his voice was gone, his gratitude rang loud and clear.

Inside, the lodge was breathtaking. A massive stone fireplace stretched to the vaulted ceiling, topped by a cow skull art piece painted by Perri. The handcrafted staircase leading to the loft was a marvel, and the freshly laid wood floors gleamed. It was a proud moment for everyone involved. Later, awards were given, and the inmates were invited back to see the completed lodge. Charlie proudly wore one of their inmate shirts that day. A moment of connection none of us will forget.

Though the full camp vision didn't materialize due to staffing challenges, Charlie's Lodge provided caregivers short-term relief and became a cherished symbol of community, faith, and love. Dave and I served as house parents to many of the children who stayed on weekends and eventually became full-time residents through the waiver process. The Lodge gave them not just shelter, but community and care. Today, twenty-five years later, the lodge is unable to house residents due to staffing shortages. Joelle—our wonderful CEO—keeps the Lodge in good shape and the license active. She even secured a grant for a new roof and sealing of the logs!

There is hope that someday it will be able to open its doors once again as a place of respite and loving care. In the meantime, Charlie's Lodge continues to serve, hosting weddings, community events, and special gatherings. What began as a dream on a wooded trail became a place of joy, rest, and hope. And every time I walk past that wooden sign, I remember the power of a community united by love, hard work, and many unforgettable weekends.

And I will never forget Charlie Daniels. His legacy at The Angelus is immeasurable. Through his generosity, music, and unwavering belief in our mission, he gave us more than we ever thought possible. Though he is no longer with us, his spirit lives on in every memory, every song, and every life he touched.

ELLIOT:
A LIFE OF UNBREAKABLE
BONDS AND QUIET COURAGE

Let me tell you about Elliot.

I didn't learn everything at once. It came in pieces, shared over time in conversations with his mother, Ruth. Well, she wasn't his biological mother, but she was the one who raised him and loved him like only a mother could.

Ruth had worked at a Catholic school in Cleveland, and one day, she told me, "We found him in the cafeteria. He'd been abandoned. Just left there... all alone." She and her husband, Dick, had always wanted a child but hadn't been able to have one of their own. "We were allowed to take him home," she said, as if the whole thing still amazed her all those years later. "There wasn't any paperwork. No birth certificate. Just love."

They raised Elliot the best they could. When they moved to Palm Harbor, they brought him with them, but things were never easy. Without a birth certificate, they couldn't get services or support, and over time, life took a hard turn. Ruth suffered a stroke that left her using a cane and unable to drive. And then Dick began to change, forgetting things, getting confused. Alzheimer's had crept in.

Ruth tried turning to her church for help, but no one knew what to do. Then, she heard about The Angelus. Because of our name, she thought we were affiliated with the Catholic Church. And while I did happen to be Catholic, I'd made sure The Angelus stayed independent so we could qualify for state funding. But all that didn't matter to her. She came through our doors simply looking for help.

At first, Elliot stayed with Ruth and Dick in their home about twenty miles south of us. But things were getting worse, fast. By the time I met him, he was painfully thin, malnourished, really. His hair had thinned to little wisps, and his big blue eyes looked too large for his pale, fragile face. He didn't walk, didn't speak, and his head and hands had a slight tremor. It was heartbreaking to see.

And yet, in the middle of all that, there was so much love. Ruth and Dick adored him. You could feel it in the way they talked to him, touched his arm, looked at him like he was the best thing that ever happened to them, even as their own health was falling apart. We didn't wait for approval or paperwork. We just took him in. He moved into Booth House, and we got to work.

Ruth and Dick still visited every weekend, without fail. But over time, Dick's condition worsened. He started getting lost, even just going to the grocery store. The police brought him home more than once. It wasn't safe anymore. Meanwhile, Elliot began having severe muscle spasms, something we learned had gone untreated for years. With help from a social worker, we got him seen by Children's Medical Services. They got him on proper medication, adjusted his diet, and before long, we started to see changes. Real ones. He was putting on weight. He was more alert. He began to thrive.

Eventually, we all had to face the truth: Ruth and Dick couldn't live alone anymore. Dick's wandering was getting dangerous, and he had to be placed in a secured memory care unit. Ruth moved into the rehab wing of the same nursing home. Their house sat empty. And then Ruth asked me something that stopped me in my tracks; she wanted me to become their legal guardian.

I didn't want to do it. I really didn't. But how could I say no?

Even after they moved into the nursing home, Ruth never stopped worrying about Elliot. So I brought him to visit her as often as I could.

Sometimes Dick would join us, too, at least in the beginning. But after the day he slipped out the front door and wandered off, that was no longer an option.

He started calling me at all hours, convinced he was having a heart attack. I'd call the nursing home, they'd rush him to the hospital, and then after a full checkup, he'd be sent right back. After a few of these episodes, I realized he didn't actually think he was dying but just needed someone to talk to. Someone who remembered who he used to be.

Ruth, on the other hand, stayed sharp. She always had a bit of mischief in her. She had a heavy smoking habit and would call me up asking for cigarettes: "Just one carton, Pauline, please," she'd say like it was a pack of gum. She ended up in trouble for handing them out to the other residents like candy.

One year for Elliot's birthday, I brought him to see her, and we threw a little party. Balloons, cake, laughter; the whole works. Elliot lit up. He swatted at the balloons with glee, and the sound of his laughter filled the room. Even the nursing home staff gathered around to watch. It was one of those moments that reminded me why we do what we do.

But it wasn't always easy. Ruth once gave her credit card to a staff member to help buy cigarettes, and it didn't go as planned. I got a call from the bank about some questionable charges, and after we got them sorted out, we had no choice but to cancel the card. Ruth was furious. She wasn't used to losing control, and she let me know it.

Around that time, we found out Dick had a brother back in Cleveland. A doctor. The social worker reached out, hoping he might be able to step in. He was shocked to hear how far things had declined, but he made one thing clear: he would not take Elliot. Apparently, when Dick and Ruth had taken Elliot in all those years ago, it had caused a rift in the family. They'd been cut off ever since. And now, decades later, the brother wasn't interested in reopening that door.

Eventually, the decision was made to sell their home and car, and Dick's brother agreed to move them back to Cleveland. But Ruth? She refused to go without Elliot. "I can't leave him," she said through tears. "He's my son."

Convincing her to let go was one of the hardest things I've ever had to do. But I knew Elliot needed to stay. He was safe at The Angelus. He was finally healthy. And most of all, he was loved. If he left, I had no idea what would happen to him.

On the day they left, Dave and I took them to the airport. The flight was tight, and the whole thing was nerve-wracking. But we got them to the gate, where Dick's brother was waiting. And then they were gone.

Elliot stayed with us. His hair grew thick and wavy, and his eyes, once so sunken, brightened with life. He laughed often—loud and joyful—and his smile became a regular part of our days. I sent Ruth photos all the time, and she wrote back, always grateful. "He looks so happy," she'd say. "That's all I ever wanted."

Dick passed away two years after they returned to Cleveland. Ruth followed six years later.

Elliot remained at The Angelus for twenty-one years. When he passed away from pneumonia, it was peaceful. He was in a place where he was known, where he belonged. He was safe. He was cherished. And in the end, that's what mattered most.

THE HAUNTED HOUSE:
FROM SCREAMS TO SPARKS

Don Surenkamp came to us one year ago with a brilliant idea. He wanted to create a haunted house at The Angelus for Halloween. With his creativity and boundless enthusiasm, he transformed our outdoor pavilion into a massive, spine-chilling haunt.

The first year was such a hit that he expanded the attraction, adding more sections and eerie elements. Live actors soon became part of the experience, hiding in the shadows, making eerie noises, and jumping out unexpectedly, sending visitors into fits of screams and laughter. These actors—mostly teenagers—were so dedicated that they arrived early, designing their own costumes and eagerly awaiting the touch of our volunteer makeup artists, who transformed them into terrifying specters.

The pavilion itself became a labyrinth of horror, divided into multiple rooms, each decorated by talented volunteers. Realistic-looking snakes, giant spiders, and gruesome scenes featuring chainsaws and coffins created a chillingly immersive experience. Even young children wanted in on the fun, so they became "cockroaches," scurrying along the floor and brushing against visitors' legs as they navigated the darkened corridors.

The haunted house quickly became one of the most celebrated Halloween attractions in Pasco County, drawing crowds from all over. The event grew into a month-long spectacle, with nightly haunts throughout October. Side attractions were added: a haunted hayride through the eerie forest, a twisted maze, and a pirate-themed "hanging scene" where unsuspecting audience members found themselves dragged into the theatrics.

Our residents played their part too. JoJo, our official greeter, set the mood at the entrance, preparing guests for their descent into darkness. Pete took up residence inside a coffin, sitting up at just the right moment to send shivers down spines. Sam, his face eerily made up, hid just inside the creaky door of a prop refrigerator, suddenly lunging out when someone dared to open it."

Every room had its own unique fright: luminescent paintings that glowed ominously, wind tunnels that howled with ghostly voices, and heart-stopping screams from unseen sources.

The event wasn't just a thrilling attraction; it was an incredible fundraiser that brought vital awareness to The Angelus. Thanks to Don and his wife, Brenda, who tirelessly recruited volunteers and masterminded the frightful scenarios, the haunted house continued for twelve unforgettable years.

Then came the devastating news: the County Fire Marshal declared that a fire sprinkler system was required for our outdoor pavilion. The cost of installation was insurmountable, and despite numerous appeals, we had no choice but to shut down our beloved haunt. The loss was heartbreaking for everyone involved.

But Don didn't let that be the end. A man of determination, he found a new way to support The Angelus. Owning a fireworks store, he pivoted to organizing a spectacular Fourth of July fireworks display. With the help of the fire department, a designated safe zone near Little John Lake became the stage for an awe-inspiring show. Don and his crew meticulously set up the fireworks while families gathered with blankets and chairs, eagerly awaiting the night's spectacle.

Over the years, the event has grown into a full-fledged celebration, complete with live music, raffles, food trucks, and vendors. By nightfall, the sky ignited with twenty-five minutes of breathtaking explosions and dazzling colors, an annual tradition that continues to captivate the community.

Don and his wife's generosity hasn't stopped there. He still surprises us, appearing as Santa Claus or even the Grinch at various events. We are endlessly grateful for their unwavering support, their dedication, and their ability to turn loss into something even more magical.

HUNTER:
A SCOUT'S JOURNEY TO EAGLE

Hunter joined The Angelus community as a polite, thoughtful young man, handsome, well-spoken, and steady in spirit. From the beginning, it was clear that he had been raised with love and care. Though I never came to know much about his early family history, it was evident he had a strong educational foundation and a quiet sense of self-respect. Due to physical challenges that required the use of full-time support and accessibility, he became a resident at Booth House, where he could live as independently as possible while still receiving the care he needed.

Hunter managed his own care with little assistance, moved freely in his wheelchair, and even handled the TV remote better than I ever could. We were able to set him up in a room near one of the smaller bathrooms which gave him just a little more privacy, which he appreciated and earned.

At Booth House, he quickly adjusted to the daily routines and got to know his housemates and caretakers. He helped with chores like setting the table for the eight residents, always taking pride in contributing. In the adult day program, he was fully engaged, bringing a quiet enthusiasm to everything he participated in.

Hunter has always loved sports, especially football. His knowledge of teams, players, and stats was impressive, and he was never far from a conversation about the Gators. Though large, noisy venues could sometimes overwhelm him, he still enjoyed going to events. I remember one time we took him to an NFL football game. Whenever there was a touchdown, cannons were blasted. Those loud booms were just too much, and we had to leave. But wrestling events? He didn't miss a second of the action, fully immersed despite the crowd's energy.

One of his proudest achievements was earning the Eagle Scout badge. He had joined a local troop and worked through the handbook with incredible focus and persistence. Badge by badge, he advanced with minimal help from staff. What made it even more special was how he shared what he learned, reading aloud to others like Frank and Jack, helping them understand the requirements. He didn't just participate, he led.

Years later, when I had already stepped back from daily operations, I was invited to attend an event where Hunter was honored for his Eagle Scout award. I'll never forget the look on his face when he was introduced, his troop leader at his side, and a room full of people standing to applaud him. He received heartfelt congratulations, thoughtful gifts, and the recognition he deserved. It was more than a ceremony. It was a moment that captured who he is: resolute, generous, and quietly extraordinary. I check in from time to time, and it warms my heart to know that Hunter is still reading to his housemates, following and cheering on his favorite sports teams, and continuing to be the calm, steady presence he's always been.

Looking back, Hunter's story reminds me of why The Angelus was created to offer not just care, but belonging, purpose, and the space for people to become their fullest selves. Hunter did that. He still does. And I'm proud to have watched his story unfold.

MARC:
A JOURNEY OF
SELF-DISCOVERY
AND QUIET TRIUMPH

Marc's parents, both dedicated pediatricians, sought a safe haven for him while they embarked on a long trip to their home in Paraguay. With two other children in tow, they knew the lengthy plane flight would be too much for little Marc, who was non-ambulatory and non-verbal but full of energy. Ever curious, Marc loved crawling around and climbing; at the lodge, he'd often make his way into the living room and happily climb into Dave's lap. Initially, he came to the lodge for short trial-run stays to see how he would adjust to being away from home.

Everything went so well that eventually his family entrusted him to our care for the duration of their trip. Marc became a permanent resident, finding a loving place in Ann House where Jack served as his unofficial guardian. He was given the freedom to explore, crawling through the living room, joining Grant on the couch, and delighting in the warm interactions of daily life. His family visited frequently, spending time with all the residents and taking Marc out for gentle walks, reassuring him with their presence.

Marc was welcomed into every event at The Angelus. During our Christmas Pageant it was nearly impossible to keep the red bow on his costume as he would eagerly grab onto anything within reach, holding on tight and refusing to let go. Often, if placed too close to another resident, he'd pull their costume toward him, eliciting smiles and laughter from the audience. Even routine tasks like haircuts presented challenges, as keeping him still for a shave was no easy feat.

As time passed, Marc's family continued to be a vital part of his life. His parents, siblings, nieces and nephews never missed a chance to sit with Uncle Marc at every Thanksgiving. Year after year the family has grown, now with grandnieces and nephews, always making sure Marc was part of every holiday. His family's unwavering support and their deep trust in The Angelus ensured that Marc was nurtured in an environment where he could be himself and thrive. His mother even became a valued member of our board of directors, offering insights that enriched our understanding of life at The Angelus.

Marc's story is one of discovery, joy, and the power of belonging. His playful nature and the love that surrounds him remind us every day why we do what we do, making our home a place where every journey is celebrated.

BOOLA BOOLA:
A JOYFUL VISITOR

In 2020, I received a call from the Pinellas County Sheriff's Office asking me to visit a trailer park in North Pinellas County. They had found an unattended child and wanted me to come prepared to take him home with me. I didn't hesitate. I grabbed a staff member, a stroller, diapers, a change of clothes, and a bungee cord just in case we needed to improvise a seatbelt. I had no idea how old he was or what we were walking into.

When we arrived, the scene was heartbreaking. Several police cars blocked off the entrance, and a group of neighbors looked on quietly as we were waved through. The trailer we approached was worn down, dimly lit, and cluttered. Inside, sitting alone on the floor, was a small boy with a beaming smile. He looked up at us as if we were expected. He offered no resistance when I scooped him into my arms. His diaper was soaked, and he wore only a shirt, but he was content and alert. I dressed him in a T-shirt that was far too big, and we changed his diaper before gently securing him in the stroller with the bungee cord.

Outside, a neighbor mentioned that his mother hadn't been home in three days. His ten-year-old sister had been doing her best to care for him. A wheelchair, dusty and stored beneath the trailer, was pulled out by a deputy and placed in our van.

We didn't know his name, but a neighbor shouted something that sounded like "Boola Boola." Until we learned otherwise, that became his name. Once at the lodge, we gave him a shower and cleaned his wheelchair thoroughly. He eagerly drank milk from a bottle and ate a processed meal with no difficulty. He was a joy to care for, and within a week, his social worker contacted us.

Boola Boola quickly charmed everyone at the lodge. Residents Mara, Boots, and JoJo enjoyed his company as he crawled on the floor and played with toys. He especially loved climbing into Dave's lap during football games, completely content to sit still and watch. He was sweet and easygoing with a cheerful presence that brought so much joy to everyone around him.

Eventually, the social worker reached out. They had located Boola Boola's grandmother in California, who agreed to care for him. Arrangements were made for a reunion. We dressed him in new clothes and brought him to the airport, where he met his grandmother and the social worker. Though he didn't seem to recognize her, she expressed gratitude for the care we had given him. While we were happy to see him reunited with family, we couldn't help but wonder how he was adjusting to his new life.

Boola Boola was only with us for a short time, but he left an imprint on all our hearts. I still think about him sometimes: his laughter, his quiet curiosity, and how we missed having him with us after he left.

EPILOGUE

THE HEART REMAINS

The Angelus brought meaning to my life, though it also demanded sacrifices, the greatest being time with my own family. I don't say that lightly. My children and grandchildren mean the world to me. But when The Angelus began, I felt called—truly called—to be present for the children and adults who lived there. They needed someone to fight for them, care for them, and build a life around them. That became my life's work. It may not have always shown on the surface how deeply I loved my family, but I did. Fiercely. I just knew how much The Angelus needed me, too, and that sometimes meant missing dinners, events, or everyday moments most mothers or grandmothers wouldn't give up. I always hoped my children understood that I showed up when it mattered most, and that my love was steady, even if it looked different from others.'

My family's involvement in The Angelus has been one of the biggest joys for me. Another is the relationships; the deep, abiding connections with the residents of The Angelus and their families. They taught me more than I could have ever given them. I gained a community, a calling, and a life filled with meaning. I saw firsthand what it means to love unconditionally, to fight for someone else's dignity, and to trust that God will make a way even when it's unclear. That has been the greatest blessing.

I wrote this book because, like me before Amber, you may never have faced a child and family in need. I hope from the stories of these incredible people that you might come to know that every life matters—no matter how difficult, different, or fragile it may seem. And I want people to know that they are capable of more than they think. We live in a world that often measures success by profit, status, or recognition. But true success is found in service. I hope that this story leaves behind a sense of possibility, a reminder that faith, love, and courage can change the world, even if only for one person at a time.

There came a moment, not long after The Angelus opened its doors, when I realized this wasn't just about providing care, it was about creating home. A home for those who had none. That changed everything. In this home, we were building family, honoring dignity, and choosing love as a daily act. That shift changed how I led, how I prayed, and how I showed up. It became my compass, and I hope it will become yours.

An epilogue is meant to tie up loose ends. But the truth is, every story you've just read has, in its own way, found a place to rest, except one: The Angelus itself.

The world has changed a great deal since we began in 1979. Life was simpler then. I could take the children on spontaneous outings. Medications were handed out in the way any parent might do at home. A scraped knee called for a Band-Aid and a hug, not a form or a protocol. We said grace before meals because it brought us peace.

But as the years passed, the systems around us evolved. Regulations increased; some necessarily, to protect those most vulnerable, and every moment of daily life became something to log and report. From medications to meals to leisurely walks, all of them must now be recorded, timed, and filed. The heart of caregiving remains, but so much of it now flows through paperwork and policy.

Staffing, too, has become more structured. Today, those who care for the residents must meet specific qualifications, complete in-service training, and navigate the demands of a field that often undervalues the depth of heart it requires. The days of live-in-house parents have passed. The homes now rely on dedicated staff professionals who bring skill and compassion, often working long hours under challenging conditions.

And still, The Angelus continues.

Though I have long since stepped back from daily operations, I remain in awe of the people who keep this vision alive. Administrators who cover shifts when no one else can. Volunteers who show up year after year. Board members who offer their wisdom and guidance. Families who entrust their loved ones to this home built from nothing but hope and determination.

The annual events—light shows, music festivals, summer picnics— have become threads in the fabric of this story. More than fundraisers, they are celebrations of belonging, milestones that remind us of how far we've come and how strong the community around The Angelus has become.

The Angelus was never just a place. It is a home. It is not just an organization. It is a family. And like any family, it continues to grow because people care enough to show up in ways both large and small.

If this book has moved you, I hope you'll carry its spirit forward. Whether through a conversation, a visit, a shared memory, or a simple act of kindness in your own community, every gesture matters. Because homes like The Angelus aren't built just once. They are sustained every day by those who believe in love, dignity, and the right to a life well lived.

ACKNOWLEDGEMENTS

First and foremost, I thank God for the strength, guidance, and grace that have carried me through every step of this journey. The Angelus was born from love, built with determination, and sustained by faith, but it has always been the people who gave it life.

To my family: your patience, sacrifices, and belief in this mission allowed me to give my whole heart to the residents of The Angelus. To my late husband, Dave, your quiet strength and unwavering love grounded me during the most uncertain times. To my children, grandchildren, and family, thank you for sharing me so generously with so many others.

A special thank you to the family members who not only supported The Angelus but also worked beside me in the service of our mission. My son Joe, whose hands-on dedication helped carry us forward through challenging times; his wife Laura, whose warmth and generosity touched every resident she continues to care for; my granddaughter Joelle, who grew up around The Angelus and stepped in as CEO with love and energy when it was time; and my daughter Perri, whose creativity, leadership, and compassion have long been woven into the very fabric of this place. Each of you gave more than your time. You gave your hearts.

And I am grateful for the energy and time that Elaine Tomasch gave during the founding of The Angelus. Her background in education brought a level of credibility and helped open certain doors in those earliest years.

To the residents—past, present, and future—you are the heart and soul of this place. You have taught us how to live with joy, how to persevere through challenges, and how to love without condition. You are why we exist.

To the families who entrusted us with their sons and daughters, brothers and sisters, thank you for your trust, your courage, and your continued support. Your partnership has meant everything.

To our staff: the caregivers, nurses, drivers, therapists, cooks, maintenance teams, and volunteers: thank you for showing up day after day with compassion and dedication. Special thanks to Aunt Lou, whose steady hands and big heart carried so much of the daily work in the early years.

To our donors, board members, and fundraising partners, you made the impossible possible. Whether it was sponsoring a room, donating supplies, or buying a ticket to an event, you helped build and sustain a place where love and dignity come first.

To our community partners, churches, businesses, and neighbors throughout Pasco County and beyond, thank you for embracing us and supporting us through every season, every challenge, and every triumph.

And to Jack, our self-appointed spokesman and constant source of joy: your voice, your stories, and your unstoppable spirit remind us daily what this place is really about. I don't need a microphone when you're around. You keep the heart of The Angelus beating strong.

There are too many names to list, but if you have ever lifted a box, played in a band, said a prayer, shared a laugh, or helped us along the way, you are part of this story. Your kindness lives in these pages and in the lives we've been privileged to touch.

With deep love and unending gratitude,
Pauline

www.ingramcontent.com/pod-product-compliance
Lightning Source LLC
Chambersburg PA
CBHW061748120626
46550CB00005B/1932